EXETER MEDIEVAL ENGLISH TEXTS AND STUDIES
General Editors: Marion Glasscoe and M.J. Swanton

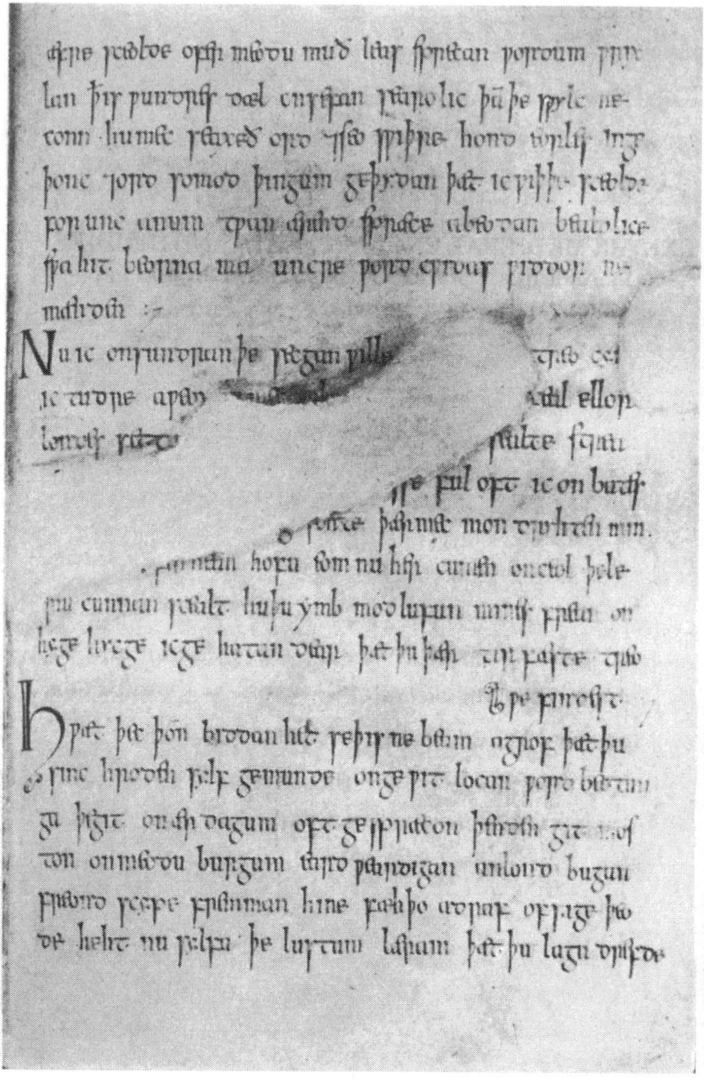

The Exeter Book, f. 123a

Three Old English Elegies

THE WIFE'S LAMENT

THE HUSBAND'S MESSAGE

THE RUIN

Edited by
R. F. LESLIE

UNIVERSITY OF EXETER

First published by Manchester University Press, 1961.

This revised edition, University of Exeter, 1988.

ISBN 978-0-85989-184-4

9 780859 891844

Printed and bound by CPI Group (UK) Ltd, Croydon, CR0 4YY

TO
ERIKA

PREFACE

ALTHOUGH the three relatively short elegiac poems in this edition have been printed many times, they are still honoured more by repute than acquaintance. Difficulties of interpretation have given rise to a considerable body of discussion, so that the poems have tended to remain the preserve of scholars rather than the property of that wider public to which their literary merit entitles them. The emphasis on the value of Old English poems as literature, which has become ever more marked during the past quarter of a century, has been made possible by the painstaking studies of several generations of scholars in the language, history and civilisation of Anglo-Saxon England. I should like to acknowledge my indebtedness to those scholars, an indebtedness particularly great in the case of the poems in this edition.

I am deeply indebted to many who have given me generously of their time and knowledge : to Dr. I. L. Gordon for reading the book in typescript and for many valuable suggestions, to Dr. F. E. Harmer for her readiness to discuss and give advice on many points, to Miss D. M. Hignett, Mr. J. E. Cross and Mr. R. W. V. Elliott for help and criticism of various aspects of the work. I wish to record my gratitude to Professor I. A. Richmond for answering my questions on the archaeology of Roman Bath, to Mr. Eric John for advice on the dating and authenticity of charters, to Miss D. Bushell, Curator of the Roman Baths at Bath, for conducting me over the remains and providing me with information, and to Miss Russ, Assistant Librarian of Bath Public Library, Mr. R. S. Wright, the former Librarian, and Dr. D. T. Donovan of the University of Bristol, for information. I wish to thank the Dean and Chapter of Exeter Cathedral for access to the manuscript and for their kind permission to reproduce folio 123a as a frontispiece, also Mrs. A. M. Erskine, Archivist of the Chapter Library, for providing the photograph. I am most grateful to Professor R. M. Wilson for his detailed help and advice since the early stages of this edition. My thanks are due to Miss B. M. Griffith for preparing the typescript for the press. My greatest indebtedness is to my wife for her advice and assistance since the inception of the work, and to

Professor G. L. Brook, who has given unsparingly of his time and knowledge from first to last, and whose indispensable advice and guidance, as General Editor of the series in which this book appears, is but the culmination of his assistance to me.

Finally, I should like to thank the Manchester University Press for undertaking the publication of the book, the Secretary, Mr. T. L. Jones, for his co-operation, and the administrators of the Ward Bequest for bearing part of the cost.

R. F. Leslie

October, 1959

ADDITIONAL PREFACE

I am greatly indebted to Professor Michael J. Swanton and The University of Exeter for undertaking to reissue my edition of *Three Old English Elegies;* the previous reprint, by Manchester University Press in 1966, went out-of-print last year.

In order to keep costs to a minimum, I have made no changes to the text. However, to make the edition as useful as possible in the circumstances, I have added a new Supplementary Bibliography for the period 1966-1987.

R. F. Leslie

October, 1987

CONTENTS

ABBREVIATIONS

AJP	*American Journal of Philology*
Archiv	*Archiv für das Studium der neueren Sprachen und Litteraturen*
Beiträge	*Beiträge zur Geschichte der deutschen Sprache und Literatur*
Bosworth-Toller or B-T	*An Anglo-Saxon Dictionary*, based on the manuscript collection of J. Bosworth, and edited and enlarged by T. N. Toller. Oxford, 1898.
Campbell	A. Campbell, *Old English Grammar*. Oxford, 1959.
ES	*Englische Studien*
Gmc.	Germanic
Grein-Köhler	Grein, C. W. M. *Sprachschatz der angelsächsischen Dichter*. Revised edition by J. J. Köhler, assisted by F. Holthausen. Heidelberg, 1912.
HM	*The Husband's Message*
JEGP, JGP	*Journal of English and Germanic Philology* (vols. i-iv under the title *Journal of Germanic Philology*).
Krapp-Dobbie	*The Exeter Book*, edited by G. P. Krapp and E. V. K. Dobbie. New York, 1936.
L	Latin
ME	Middle English
MLN	*Modern Language Notes*
MLR	*Modern Language Review*
MP	*Modern Philology*
OE	Old English
OHG	Old High German
ON	Old Norse
OS	Old Saxon
pp.	past participle

PMLA	*Publications of the Modern Language Association of America*
PQ	*Philological Quarterly*
R	*The Ruin*
Sievers- Brunner	*Altenglische Grammatik nach der Angelsächsischen Grammatik von E. Sievers*, revised by K. Brunner. Second edition. Halle, 1951.
sv.	strong verb
Toller	*An Anglo-Saxon Dictionary Supplement* by T. N. Toller. Oxford, 1921.
w.	with
wk.	weak
WGmc.	West Germanic
WL	*The Wife's Lament*
WS	West Saxon
wv.	weak verb
ZfdA	*Zeitschrift für deutsches Altertum und deutsche Litteratur*

INTRODUCTION

THE MANUSCRIPT

THE three poems in this edition have been preserved in *The Exeter Book*, an anthology compiled towards the end of the tenth century and containing the most varied collection of the poetry which survives from Anglo-Saxon times. *The Wife's Lament* on folios 115*a* and *b* is separated by a number of short religious poems and two riddles from *The Husband's Message* on folios 123*a* and *b*, which is followed immediately by *The Ruin* on folios 123*b*-124*b*. Portions of text are missing from the last two poems in lines 8-13 on both sides of folios 123 and 124 as a result of damage generally attributed to a burning fragment of wood falling on to the back of the MS. and eating its way into the book.

The MS. was given to Exeter Cathedral by Leofric, the first bishop of Exeter, who died in 1072. It has since remained in the Chapter Library (press mark No. 3501) except for two short periods, during which reproductions were made at the British Museum. The first of these was a pen and ink transcript of the whole (B.M. Additional MS. 9067) made, according to Wülker,[1] in 1831 by a Robert Chambers, of whom very little is known. This was collated with the MS. in 1832 by Sir Frederic Madden, according to an inscription in the transcript itself, and is of some assistance in the reading of letters at the edges of the lacunae where fragments seem to have disappeared during the century or so since the transcript was made. The MS. was once more transferred to the British Museum in 1930, when a collotype facsimile was made, the damaged folios repaired and the MS. rebound. The facsimile, published in 1933 with introductory chapters by R. W. Chambers, Max Förster and Robin Flower, contains a comprehensive description and detailed palaeographical analysis of the MS.

There are no sectional divisions in *The Wife's Lament* and *The Ruin*, but *The Husband's Message* is divided into three parts. The last section, which begins at line 26, is just over

---

[1] *Grundriss zur Geschichte der angelsächsischen Litteratur* (Leipzig, 1885), p. 222.

twice as long as the first two, which are of almost equal length. Since two riddles precede the poem, it is not unlikely that *The Husband's Message* too was at one time mistaken for three separate riddles. (See pp. 13-14.)

THE ELEGIAC FORM

The three poems in this edition have given rise to endless discussion of their form and meaning, mainly because they present situations without localisation of the settings or identification of the characters. The fondness of Anglo-Saxon poets for generalisation may be seen in *The Fortunes of Men*, in the series of gnomic verses known as *Maxims* I and II, and in many passages from poems with otherwise specific settings such as the elegy of the last survivor in *Beowulf*, lines 2247-66 and the father's lament in lines 2444-62 of the same poem. In accordance, therefore, with this habit of generalisation, the three poems might be regarded as studies in the expression of atmosphere, emotions and principles of behaviour, the characters and backgrounds being little more than sketched in, with no more substance than is necessary for the immediate situation. Each poem, however, contains sufficient concrete detail to make it clear that it is founded on a particular experience. Since they lack named characters and the precisely stated social and historical contexts of poems such as *Beowulf*, the key to their interpretation is to be found in a fuller understanding of the semantic overtones of those words and phrases which appear to have had a deep social or aesthetic significance for the Anglo-Saxons ; examples of these are *folgað* and *fæhðu* in *The Wife's Lament* 9 and 26, and the stereotyped phrases in *The Wife's Lament* 1-3, *The Husband's Message* 21-3 and *The Ruin* 1-2, all of which are discussed from this point of view in the following pages.

It seems probable that the poems contain within themselves the clues to their elucidation, but our remoteness in time and way of life from Anglo-Saxon England must make us wish that the writers had been rather more explicit. An examination of the structure of the poems, however, makes it clear that any increase in the purely informative content would weaken their dramatic impact, and that their literary merit lies precisely in the balance struck between delineation of character and situation on the one hand, and the evocation of an elegiac mood on the other.

The Ruin stands rather apart from the other two poems ; its theme is an imaginative nostalgia for a glorious past, stimulated by a particular scene spread out before the poet's eyes. Both *The Wife's Lament* and *The Husband's Message* are psychological studies. They contain too much detail for them to be readily explained as lyric passages isolated from longer poems and, at first sight, too little to allow them to stand by themselves. In view of their allusive style and the wealth of meaning packed into words and phrases, the answer to the problem may well be that the characters and their circumstances owe their truth to the fact that they represent typical situations in which the emotions they call forth can be most powerfully displayed. The enmity of the husband's kin towards the wife in *The Wife's Lament* and the necessity for the husband to send a messenger instead of coming himself for his wife in *The Husband's Message* are then seen to be, not loose ends, but circumstances enhancing the particular dilemma which is the starting-point for each of the elegiac studies.

THE WIFE'S LAMENT

This poem has often been called a dramatic monologue. It is one of the few poems in Old English literature dealing with the relationship between man and woman, and the only comprehensive study of a woman's thoughts and feelings. The main theme is the bitterness of separation as seen from her point of view. That the speaker is a woman is clear from the feminine forms in the opening lines, a fact ignored or disregarded by the earliest editors. Some critics have held that the woman speaks of two men in the poem : a lover referred to in lines 18-26 and 42-52, and her husband else-where in the poem. This view has rested principally on the abrupt changes in tone and on the variety of terms for ' man '. The breaks in continuity, however, are completely consistent with the ebb and flow of the woman's feelings. Just at those points where her sorrow and loneliness are most vividly present to her in lines 5, 14, 25-6 and 39-41, after rising to a crescendo in the preceding lines, she reverts from the effect to

the cause. When she can no longer endure the intensity of
her present distress she steadies herself with the contemplation
of what is past. The variation of her terms for ' man ' is in
keeping with the subject of her monologue. The man whom
she calls her lord in lines 6, 8, 15 and 33 is referred to in more
formal terms in objective narrative passages, just as the *ful
gemæcne monnan* of line 18 is simply the man with whom she
had exchanged vows. In the emotionally charged closing
passage she is concerned rather with her personal relationship
to the man than with her formal association with him ; here
he appears as her friend and lover (47, 49, 50). Since her
terminology varies in accordance with her attitude, probability
favours the identification of her lover with her lord, especially
since she sorrows for her lord who is abroad (5-7), and also
shows deep concern and longing for her lover who is *feorres
folclondes . . . wætre beflowen* (47-9). The striking similarity
of situation points to these references being to one and the
same man. Finally, it cannot be argued that sorrow for her
absent lord is driven from her mind by another man whom
she mentions meeting in lines 18-26, since she states in lines
30-3 that her lord's departure has often caused her distress
in the place and condition from which she utters her lament.
The key words are *oft* and *hēr* (32). The *ūhtceare* (7) which
she suffered about her lord's whereabouts is that which she
enlarges upon, in a speculation coloured with her own suffer-
ings (45-51), when she paints a picture of his probable circum-
stances.

If the woman's sorrow is for one man, is he her husband?
Frēond (47) is also used in a comparable context in *Maxims*
II 44, where it refers to a man whom a woman desires to have
as a husband. Elsewhere in Old English poetry compounds
of *frēond* when used of men and women indicate married love,[1]
and *frēondscipe* in line 25 is likely to be love between husband
and wife, for it is used of the conjugal relationship in *The
Husband's Message* 19. To describe her formal relationship to
him she uses both *hlāford* (6, 15) and *frēan* (33). The latter
is used of Wealhþēow's husband Hrōðgār in *Beowulf* 641,
many times in the Old English poem *Genesis*, and in *Maxims*
I 84-92, where the duties of a prince's wife are listed. Her

---

[1] As in *frēondmynde (Genesis* 1831), *frēondlufu (ibid.* 1834), and
frēondrǣdenne (Juliana 34, 71).

avowal of him as her *hlāford* is significant, for this is the tech-
nical term for the relationship in which a nobleman stands to
his retainers, and in the Anglo-Saxon Laws the status of a
wife is similar to that of a retainer.[1]

The story of the poem is highly condensed, and subordin-
ated completely to the emotional pattern woven by the
woman's feelings. Many explanations of her situation have
been advanced, but insufficient importance has generally been
attached to the structural pattern of the poem, attention to
which narrows the field for speculation, even though it does
not entirely eliminate possible ambiguities.

The poem opens with a conventional formula indicating
the elegiac nature of what is to follow.[2] Line 6 begins a
narrative passage in which she indicates the origin of her
troubles, her lord's departure overseas. She gives no reason
for this, unlike the messenger in *The Husband's Message*, who,
in lines 19-20, specifically mentions exile as the cause of the
husband's departure. There are, however, hints that the
husband's departure in *The Wife's Lament* was forced ; the
use of *unc* and *wit* (12-13) indicates that the conspiracy of his
kin is directed against both husband and wife, who are to live
far apart and in as wretched a condition as possible (13-14).
That the plot succeeds is evidenced by her own wretched
plight (27 ff.), and by her picture of the imagined desolation
and loneliness in which her husband is living (47-52). There
is reason to believe that he is unlikely to return ; the plot to
keep them far apart depends on keeping him away, for the
wife's suffering takes place in her husband's land, as is shown
by the adverbs she uses. She states that he has gone ' hence ',
heonan, from his people (6), that she has been prevented from
leaving (9 ff.), and that she has been banished to a lonely spot
(27 ff.) which is ' here ' (*hēr*, line 32) where she utters her
lament. These adverbs refute the suggestion made in the most
recent discussion of the problems of the poem,[3] that having
exiled herself to a foreign land, she is there banished to the
wilderness. So also does line 15, which has been taken as a

[1] F. Liebermann, *Die Gesetze der Angelsachsen* (Halle, 1906), ii. 370,
s.v. *Eheschliessung*, 8*i*.
[2] Cf. *The Seafarer* 1-2, *Beowulf* 1065, 1723-4, 2108, 2154, 2446,
Vainglory 15, *Juliana* 719, *The Order of the World* 12.
[3] S. B. Greenfield, ' *The Wife's Lament* Reconsidered ', *PMLA*, lxviii
(1953), 907 ff.

reference to the cruelty of the woman's husband in ordering her confinement in her grim surroundings. However, this line cannot refer to her present plight at all, for the present tense *āh* would be required in line 16, not the preterite *āhte* which occurs, especially if she were confined in a land other than her husband's. The emphatic use of ' this ' in the phrase *on þissum londstede* (16) certainly implies, as Greenfield suggests, that she has known another land ; but it was her own native land which she left for this of her husband. With the reading *eard* for MS. *heard*, not only the linguistic but the contextual difficulties of lines 15-17 can be resolved. Her lord bade her take up her abode in this land ; she had no faithful friends here (as she had in her homeland) ; therefore her heart is sad (because her loneliness was great when her husband left).

Lines 18-26 follow logically on her reflections in the preceding lines. After settling in a strange land she found that her husband, apparently at first a congenial mate (18), was ill-starred, troubled in spirit, concealing his thoughts and contemplating either murder or some other crime (19-20). This discovery cannot follow the events in lines 6-14. If her husband were already abroad and the crime or murder were directed against her, she would know of its effects, not its contemplation, and there would be no point in the phrase *mōd mīþendne* (20). As regards her own suffering, she must hold her husband guiltless since she has already shown her awareness that her banishment was part of a plot by her husband's kin after he had gone (11-14). The *morþor* which she had discovered him to be meditating must have been directed against someone else, and it furnishes one explanation for his departure abroad. We are told further that he cloaked his intentions under a cheerful demeanour (21) ; such behaviour can be explained by a desire to avoid giving his wife any uneasiness, for he would know that ignorance of his proposed crime would be necessary to her if she were to be spared the consequences of it ; a wife could suffer, because of fore-knowledge of the commission of a crime, the same penalty as her husband would incur.[1]

In lines 25-6 she states that she must suffer far or near the *fǣhðu* of her beloved. This word is taken by some

---

[1] Cf. Liebermann, *op. cit.* i. 644.

scholars, including Greenfield, as important evidence that she is the victim of her husband's hostility ; but *fǣhðu* always denotes a state of feud (see Notes) ; it is a technical term, like *folgað* in line 9, of whose overtones and compression the poet avails himself in order to avoid the necessity for digression and distraction from the major theme of the woman's emotions. Love has not been turned to hate ; a vow never to be parted has been rendered null by the husband's feud, which will now be visited upon her, an eventuality which he had striven to avoid (20-1), but which gave the conspirators (11-12) an opportunity to procure her banishment, thus preventing her from following him abroad, her undoubted intention in the much discussed phrase *folgað sēcan* (9). Since *folgað* has invariably the technical sense of service due to a lord by his retainers, and since the wife stood in the same relation to her husband as a retainer, there is a strong case for taking *folgað* as her duty to him as a wife. It reinforces the lord and retainer image raised by *mīn lēodfruma* in line 8. The conventional exile imagery which follows in line 10 reinforces the impression that the retainer aspect of her relationship is emphasised because of its central position in the Anglo-Saxon elegiac tradition, as instanced in *The Wanderer* and elsewhere. She is in fact exiled from her husband's company ; her *wēapearfe* (10) is for his presence, for which she shows her longing in line 14.

With line 26 ends the woman's reversion to the events of former days. In lines 27-41 she returns to the outcome of the kinsmen's plot against her. She is ordered to live in a cave or tumulus in the woods in wild and solitary surroundings which she goes on to describe. Greenfield restates a general belief that in this passage is portrayed the execution of the husband's order to imprison his wife in the wilds, and claims that it follows logically the command in line 15. If this were so, it is not clear why she should make a second reference to her sentence of banishment without any indication of the agent, for the construction of line 27 is impersonal. The commands in lines 15 and 27 are no doubt consciously related to each other, but the relationship is one of antithesis, to stress the contrast between her former happier state and her present plight. In the first passage she obeyed as a wife, in the second she was despatched as an outcast.

Despite their importance, there has been little agreement
on the meaning of lines 42 ff. The formula *Ā scyle . . . sceal
. . .* is undoubtedly gnomic (see Notes), that is, one used to
introduce a passage of generalised reflections or maxims. The
geong mon is an impersonal figure ; he does not represent the
woman's husband as has recently been suggested,[1] but the
woman herself, for the generalised *mon* could be used of women
as well as men (see Bosworth-Toller, s.v. *mann* I). The use
of the subjunctive has led to the whole passage being taken as
a curse by the woman upon either a lover or her husband ;
but the indicative verbs in lines 47-51 do not suggest a situa-
tion which she desires for her husband, but one in which he is,
or could be, placed. Moreover, the phrase *ā scyle* indicates
desirable conduct, as it does in *Maxims* I 177-8 and *Maxims* II
54-5, not a state of mind in which she desires her husband to
be. On the contrary, she is, in lines 42-45a, attempting to
sustain her own morale by reflections on the virtue of for-
titude after the note of hopelessness on which the previous
passage ends. A young person, she says, must be grave and
stouthearted; likewise she must have a cheerful demeanour
together with her heartache, her host of constant sorrows.[2]

A new sentence begins at line 45b with the first *sȳ* opening
a subordinate clause correlative with the *sȳ* clause in line 46b ;
inversion of the subject and verb in line 50b reveals the
principal clause on which both depend (see Notes to lines
45b-47). The woman's picture of her husband's plight may
be an imagined one, but she believes one or other of her
hypotheses to be true, probably the latter since she gives it in
greater detail ; hence the use of the indicative in the subor-
dinate clause in lines 47b-50a : ' Whether all his joy in the
world is dependent on himself (i.e. whether he has control of
his own destiny) or whether it is as an outcast . . . that my
beloved sits beneath a cliff . . . that friend of mine suffers
much grief. Too often he recalls a happier abode.' It is the
vividness of her portrayal of him which brings back to her the
pain of separation and accounts for the closing cry of longing.

[1] Greenfield, *loc. cit.* p. 911, n. 1.
[2] J. A. Ward, in ' *The Wife's Lament* : An Interpretation ', *JEGP*
lix (1960), 32, believes that these lines refer to one of her enemies,
possibly the leader of the rebellious forces who overthrew her lord.
This article, and that by Robert D. Stevick, appeared too late for
consideration in the Introduction itself.

Sources

It has frequently been suggested that *The Wife's Lament* is only a fragment of a much longer narrative poem, owing its preservation to its emotional interest, and that it contains a condensed and allusive version of a story known to us from other sources. The widely-distributed Constance or ' banished wife ' tale has been put forward as a source, particularly in the form which it took in legends referring to Offa, king of Mercia from 757 to 796, as recounted in a Latin work of about 1200 from St. Albans (Cotton MS. Nero D I).[1] Here Offa's wife is the suffering patient heroine who marries a foreign prince, is banished with her children, but in the end happily rejoins her husband. Children feature in all variants of the Constance tale, but there is no mention of them in our poem; nor is there, as in the Offa variant, any mention of the woman earning her living while in exile, or of the hermit with whom Offa's wife takes refuge ; indeed the woman's loneliness is stressed. The mother-in-law is prominent as the persecutor in many versions of the tale, and Miss Rickert sees her as one of the *monnes māgas* (11), acting through male relatives ; but the subordinate and undifferentiated role played by the husband's kin in the poem is difficult to reconcile with the mother-in-law's role in the presumed source.

The Crescentia tale of the exiled queen has been proposed as a source by S. Stefanovíc, although the possibility of this tale being known in Europe early enough has been disputed.[2] In one particular, this tale is closer to our poem than the Constance story ; there are no children. But there are objections, of which the first is the necessity of introducing a seducer in lines 18-26 and of taking lines 42-5 as an imprecation upon him. There is further the assumption that the woman finds her husband after she departs *folgað sēcan* (9) in order to clear herself of a charge of infidelity reported to her

[1] The principal exponent is Miss Edith Rickert, ' The Old English Offa Saga ', *MP* ii (1904-5), 365 ff.

[2] See S. Stefanovíc, ' Das Angelsächsische Gedicht *Die Klage der Frau* ', *Anglia*, xxxii (1909), 398-433, also A. Wallensköld, *Le Conte de la Femme Chaste Convoitée par son Beau-Frère* (Helsingfors, 1909), p. 80, and Stefanovíc's reply in *Romanische Forschungen*, xxix (1910-11), 461-556.

absent husband by his younger brother who had sought in vain to seduce her. There is no indication of infidelity in the poem, nor does the woman leave to rebut an accusation ; it is only as she is on the point of departure to seek her husband that the man's kin actively conspire against her. Lines 47-50 are taken by Stefanovíc to refer to the husband ; if, however, she is assumed to have met him and to have been banished by him, her ignorance of his circumstances is surprising.

R. Imelmann's theory of an Anglo-Saxon Odoaker saga,[1] of which *The Wife's Lament*, *Wulf and Eadwacer*, *The Husband's Message*, *The Wanderer*, and *The Seafarer* are all part, is based on the adventures of a fifth-century Continental Saxon of that name at the time of the expansion of the Saxons and their attempts to found a kingdom on the north coast of France. In support of one episode our poem is quoted ; in support of another, quotations from *The Husband's Message* are adduced as evidence. He does not first establish a relationship between the two poems ; but, in attempting to prove the interrelationship of the poems, he assumes that relationship. Other attempts to prove that these two poems are parts of the same story, are discussed in the introduction to *The Husband's Message*, pages 18-19. A major stumbling-block in the way of all theories of an origin in a well-known tale is the complete absence of proper names, an objection which applies to the recently suggested analogue in Old Irish, the poem *Liadain & Curithir*,[2] which, with its portrayal of the feelings of a man and woman separated by exile, evokes a response similar to that of *The Wife's Lament*.

THE POEM

The primary purpose of the poet has been to evoke a mood, not to tell a story. Less than a third of the poem is devoted to the facts of the woman's situation. Events are starkly presented in a highly condensed fashion ; they are not unfolded chronologically but in an order which subordinates them to the dramatic expression of the woman's lament and brings them in at points appropriate to the flux of her feelings

[1] *Forschungen zur Altenglischen Poesie* (Berlin, 1920), pp. 1-38 *et al.*
[2] G. W. Dunleavy, ' Possible Irish Analogues for *The Wife's Lament* ', *PQ*, xxxv (1956), 208-13.

of grief and longing. There is no relaxation of tension, yet the poem is preserved from excess and monotony by a skilful alternation of subjective and objective passages, and by a variation in emphasis in the two distinct and almost equal sections into which it can be divided. The first contains almost all the narrative, told simply and austerely, but punctuated by terse expressions of intense longing which underline the action without impeding it.

In the second part of the poem narrative is restricted to the opening lines (27-8), which usher in the present situation. Much of the rest describes the woman's environment and emotions and their complex interaction. Her agony of mind is deepened by the gloom and hostility of nature in her place of exile (27-32). But her surroundings are not only desolate in themselves ; she has invested them with something of her own desolation of spirit, summed up in *wic wynna lēas* (32). The same interplay of emotion and environment is evident in an early Welsh elegy of exile.[1] In the closing passage her surroundings colour her picture of her husband's imagined situation. He may be surrounded by water, as she is by briars; both water and briars appear to be symbols of the separation of each from the other. Briars, thorns and brambles are similarly used as elegiac motifs in early Welsh and Irish poetry. The Irish Queen Gormflaith refers to them when contrasting her former royal state with the miserable condition in which she is when she utters the poem.[2] In the Welsh elegy on Urien they overrun the hearth of Rheged.[3] He too must recall a happier place, *wynlicran wic* (52), a phrase which recalls her own *wic wynna lēas*. As in the first half, each passage ends on a highly personal note, but one that is now sustained and more passionate.

A remarkable feature of the poem is the regularity with which each passage is rounded off with outbursts of feeling which become in places almost refrains. There is, moreover, a parallelism between these echoing phrases at the ends of corresponding passages in each half : in lines 14 and 29,

[1] Translated and discussed by K. Jackson in *Early Celtic Nature Poetry* (Cambridge, 1935), pp. 53-6 and 114.
[2] O. J. Bergin, *Miscellany Presented to Kuno Meyer* (Halle, 1912), p. 352.
[3] Ifor Williams, *Canu Llywarch Hen* (Cardiff, 1935), pp. 18-19.

which conclude narrative sections, and in lines 17 and 39-41, which conclude reflections on her friendless state.[1]

A dominant note is struck by the word *longaþ* and related forms. The blend of grief and longing in this word appears at points of dramatic and emotional intensity in lines 14, 29, 41, 53, always at the close of a passage, always with increasing emphasis, until it culminates in that last bitter cry of hopeless longing which, by its gnomic phrasing rises from her own particular case to embrace all lovers who are parted.

Other echoes and parallel phrases emphasise focal points in the woman's orientation of her feelings. The near repetition of *under āctrēo in þām eorðscræfe* (28) in line 36 indicates how deeply the nature of her dwelling has branded itself on her mind. Her awareness of it as the fixed setting for her actions and behaviour is emphasised by the balanced phrasing of *þǣr ic sittan mōt* (37) and *þǣr ic wēpan mæg* (38). Her conviction of her husband's mental suffering, regardless of his physical state, is indicated in the antithesis introduced by *sȳ . . . sȳ . . .* (45 ff.).

Such plot as there is appears to be designed, as in *The Wanderer*, to indicate the depths of misery and adversity that man can be called upon to endure : in the case of a man, loss of his lord and the hardships of exile, in the case of a woman, desertion by her husband and rejection by his kin in a strange land. As with her male counterpart, acceptance of a harsh fate does not breed a cold stoicism. Her passionate nature and vivid imagination refuse her the consolation of self-deception. Her intensity of feeling, her honesty, her fortitude without hope, these are qualities which both ennoble and deepen her sufferings.

THE HUSBAND'S MESSAGE

Like *The Wife's Lament* this poem is a monologue, but it takes the form of a message from a nobleman, driven abroad by a feud, addressed directly to the wife whom he has left behind. That a woman of rank is being addressed can be

---

[1] cf. Robert D. Stevick's ' Formal Aspects of *The Wife's Lament* ', *JEGP*, lix (1960), 21-5, which has appeared since this edition was set in print.

inferred from the adjective *sinchroden* (14), a frequent attribute of noble women in Old English, and the phrase *pēodnes dohtor* (48). The main theme is an appeal by the husband to his wife, through a messenger, to come away and rejoin him across the sea in exile now that he has repaired his fortunes and can offer her a position and degree of prosperity commensurate with that which the two of them had enjoyed in days gone by.

One of the principal difficulties of interpretation is the point at which the poem begins. There are no titles in the manuscript and we cannot rely entirely on the scribe's practice of beginning a new poem with a new line and a capital letter, since he divides long poems, and sometimes shorter ones, into sections where there is a change of tone or topic. Between the poem entitled *Homiletic Fragment* II by Krapp-Dobbie and *The Ruin* there are five passages of verse, each containing or consisting of an address. The last three are so closely linked in subject matter that there has been general agreement that they constitute all or part of one poem to which the title of *The Husband's Message* has been given. The first of the five sections was identified by Grein as a repetition of Riddle 30, appearing earlier in the same manuscript, and he suggested that the second piece was also a riddle.[1] It is now generally referred to as Riddle 60, to which the solution ' reed ' is given.[2] Some scholars, however, have denied that it is a riddle and have followed Blackburn in considering it to be the opening section of *The Husband's Message*,[3] on the grounds that in the last four lines the speaker refers to itself as a message in writing, as does the piece of wood bearing an inscription in *The Husband's Message*. This inscribed wood or rune-stave, it is claimed, expresses in its own person the contents of our poem.

There are, however, a number of references in the text which appear to militate against the speaker being a rune-stave personified, and which support his identification as a human messenger. First, he has been in the habit of making frequent voyages (6), behaviour not reconcilable with a

[1] *Bibliothek der Angelsächsischen Poesie*, i. 246 ; ii. 397, 409.

[2] F. Tupper (Jr.), *The Riddles of the Exeter Book* (Boston, 1910), p. 199.

[3] F. Blackburn, ' *The Husband's Message* and the accompanying Riddles of *The Exeter Book* ', *JGP*, iii. (1901), 1-13.

particular rune-stave, whose significance is for the one voyage from the husband to his wife. Secondly, the speaker's reference to the man *sē þisne bēam āgrōf* (13) suggests that the speaker and the rune-stave are not one and the same person, especially since the speaker has already referred to himself directly as *mec* in line 3. Thirdly, the terms he uses of his master, *mondryhten mīn* (7), *mīnes frēan* (10) and *mīn wine* (39), indicate a lord and retainer relationship with which the limited and temporary nature of a rune-stave appears incompatible. Finally, in lines 30 ff. the speaker is recounting what the husband told him—*þæsþe hē mē sægde* (31) ; the verb *sægde* is much more appropriate to a human messenger than to a rune-stave whose function is essentially the conveyance of a written message.

Although the mutilated state of the first five lines prevents an exact assessment of the relevance of the opening of the poem, it is likely that *trēocyn* (2) refers to the rune-stave, the *þisne bēam* of line 13, which the messenger has handed over to the woman, and which serves to authenticate him as coming from her lord. It has been claimed that the opening word *nū* implies the beginning of a new passage, not the commencement of a poem.[1] It seems, however, to be a legitimate opening word, serving as a means of attracting attention in poems where an audience is directly addressed, as in *The Exhortation to Christian Living*, *Cædmon's Hymn* and the opening of the address in *The Judgement Day* II, 26. Moreover, if the rune-stave has just been presented, *nū* follows naturally as an introduction to the messenger's account of his connection with the woman's husband and the circumstances which have led to his coming. After the introductory reference to the rune-stave, he appears to be discussing his lineage (2-3a), then his functions and travels as an envoy (6-8a) ; lines 8b-12a introduce the specific errand on which he has come, and contain a summary of the theme of the whole poem.

It is difficult to believe that the whole of *The Husband's Message* could have been engraved on a rune-stave, as earlier scholars maintained. So much is conceded by Elliott, who nevertheless deems the poem to be an explanation of the terse

[1] R. W. V. Elliott, ' The Runes in *The Husband's Message* ', *JEGP*, liv (1955), 2.

runic message at the end, in greatly expanded form, which
' allows the inclusion of the wood's history as well as the more
detailed exposition of the actual situation of husband and
wife and the message sent by the former '.[1] To assume such
duplication, however, is to complicate the issue of the poem
by yoking an unreal situation, the rune-stave's imagined
speech, to a real situation, the husband's actual message.
Moreover, the impact of the runic message is thereby lessened,
and it becomes simply a summary of what has gone before.
The runes come at the end of the poem where one expects a
climax rather than a recapitulation.

MEANING OF THE RUNES

The punctuation of the runes in the MS. has been held to
indicate that they are to be read separately rather than in a
group or groups ;[2] but in Riddle 24, in which the runes com-
bine to form a word, they are preceded and followed by a stop
as they are here. The runes in *The Husband's Message* are
S, R, EA, W and probably M. The last is written somewhat
ambiguously and is sometimes read as D ; but it has the same
form as the rune in *The Ruin* 23, which must be M since it
forms the first element of the compound noun *mondrēama*,
with *m* required for alliteration.

Attempts have been made to combine the letters into one
word, as in many rune riddles. By transposing R and W,
Sedgefield obtains *sweard*, a possible variant of *sweord*, ' sword '
or ' swearing ' ;[3] but the runes are the object of the verb
gehȳre and are followed by *benemnan*, so that they must denote
a person or personified object. Hicketier reads the runes in
reverse order to obtain the proper name *Dwears*, which he
relates to OE *pweorh*.[4] His phonology is unconvincing and, as
he admits, the name is not found in Old English.

Miss Kershaw suggests that the runes represent the initials
of five personal names,[5] and Trautmann that they are the

[1] *loc. cit.* p. 5.
[2] Krapp-Dobbie, *The Exeter Book* (New York, 1936), pp. 363-4 ;
Elliott, *loc. cit.* p. 2.
[3] *An Anglo-Saxon Verse-Book* (Manchester, 1922), p. 159.
[4] ' *Klage der Frau, Botschaft des Gemahls*, und *Ruine* ', *Anglia*, xi
(1889), 365-6.
[5] *Anglo-Saxon and Norse Poems* (Cambridge, 1922), p. 42, n. 2.

initial letters of elements in compound names such as *Sigerēd*
and *Ealdwine*, with M by itself to form the name *Mon* or
Monna.[1] But Elliott has shown that if a group of runes like
the present does not spell a word, it can be interpreted cor-
rectly only by giving to each rune its name.[2] Four of the
rune names are straightforward : *sigel* ' sun ', *rād* ' path ',
wyn ' joy ', and *mann* ' man '. The fifth, *ēar*, could have two
ranges of meaning : ' ocean, sea, wave ' or ' earth, soil,
gravel '. Kock had already followed this procedure, combin-
ing S and R to read *sigelrād*, ' sun's road, heaven ', EA and W
to read *eardwynn* ' the lovely earth ', and taking M as *mon*.[3]
Elliott takes *sigelrād* as referring to the southward journey to
be undertaken by the woman, indicated in lines 27b-28. The
remaining runes he takes separately. *Ēar* refers to the sea
crossed by the husband on his way to exile and now to be
traversed by his wife going to meet him, and *wynn* to the joy
of reunion. If the last rune is *dæg*, then the vows of *ǣrdagum*
(16, 54) are indicated ; if it is *mon*, then the husband himself
is meant. In short, Elliott sees the runes as epitomising the
main themes of the poem, which are presented in expanded
form by the rune-stave personified. The presence of *geador*
(50) confirms that S and R should be taken together as a
compound noun, *sigelrād*. The sentence *woruldcandel scān*,
sigel sūðan fūs in *Beowulf* 1965-6 appears to sanction the use
of the sun as an indication of direction, but the second part
of the compound, *-rād*, should indicate the element of *sigel*,
' the sun ', by analogy with the kennings *swanrād* and *hronrād*,
which refer to the sea. *Sigelrād* is, therefore, to be inter-
preted as ' sky '. As for EA and W, since they are linked by
the same punctuation as S and R, they should also be read as
a compound, *ēarwyn*. Although *ēar* by itself can mean ' sea '
or ' earth ', the compound is probably ' the lovely earth ' on
the analogy of similarly constructed compound words and
phrases such as *ēðelwyn*, *eorðan wyn* and *eardlufu*. If these
words, along with M for *mon*, are read in conjunction with
gehȳre, then the messenger says of the ancient vows of the

---

[1] ' Zur *Botschaft des Gemahls* ', *Anglia*, xvi (1894), 221 ; likewise
C. W. Kennedy, *The Earliest English Poetry* (Oxford, 1943), pp. 123-4.
[2] *loc. cit.* p. 3.
[3] 'Interpretations and Emendations of Early English Texts :
VIII ', *Anglia*, xlix (1921), 122-3.

husband and wife (49) : ' I hear heaven, earth and the man declare together by oath that he would implement those pledges and those vows of love which you two often voiced in days gone by.' He uses the present tense for vividness, in recalling an event at which he himself has been present. The husband's actual words had probably been put in such a traditional form as ' I call upon heaven and earth to witness that I shall remain true to my vows. . . .'. These are the sacred elemental names,[1] which may be coupled with his own on the rune-stave and names by which they had in all probability both sworn their *eald gebēot* (49) *þe git on ǣrdagum oft gesprǣconn* (54). The last line is an exact repetition of line 16, where the *wordbēotunga* of husband and wife are recalled in the same passage as the only direct reference to the rune-stave, a passage containing the text of the message which the husband had commanded his messenger to relate. The repetition of line 16 is not accidental or fortuitous ; it underlines the reciprocal nature of their vows, twice mentioned in connection with the rune-stave, whose contents when disclosed at the end serve by their runic form to underline the sacred and solemn nature of the vows which the husband has now re-affirmed.

The presence of the runes may have been in part responsible for the scribal division of this short poem into three sections, lines 1-12, 13-25, 26-54. As was first suggested by Ettmüller, the scribe may have believed that he was dealing with three riddles, since the poem is preceded and followed, after *The Ruin*, by riddles. Runes are used in a number of the riddles of the Exeter Book collection. The presence of the runes does not, however, explain the first two divisions. Yet lines 2 and 3 of the poem, with their reference to the origins and upbringing of the speaker, are reminiscent of the riddle technique, and, on a cursory reading, *trēowe findest* at

---

[1] Cf. the formula of the oath whereby Irish kings in pagan times bound themselves in matters of great moment by taking to witness the sun, moon and other elements, a form of oath which survived for a time, with modifications, the introduction of Christianity (C. S. Boswell, *An Irish Precursor of Dante* (London, 1908), p. 21). In an Irish poem, edited by R. Thurneysen, the tenth strophe reads: ' These are the oaths which they pledged—the sky, the earth, the moon, the bright sun, that they would have their will from height to height, as long as the sea encompasses Ireland.' (*Zeitschrift für Celtische Philologie*, xi (1917), 58) ; traced with the kind assistance of Professor Dillon.

the end of the section could have been taken to refer back to
trēocyn in line 2, although the former refers to ' truth ' and
the first element of the compound means ' tree '.   Although
the second section has not a riddle form, its superficial resem-
blance in theme to Riddles 30 and 60 and to the first section
of our poem—it opens with *bēam* and has *bearwe* near the end
in line 23—may have served to confirm a transcriber in the
view that he had to do with a series of tree or plant riddles.

SOURCES

The theory that this poem and *The Wife's Lament* are part
of the same tale has been supported by a number of scholars.[1]
There is nothing in the plot of *The Wife's Lament* as inter-
preted above that is incompatible with the situation in *The
Husband's Message*, but it has not been conclusively shown
that they must be parts of the same story.   Vows of fidelity
are mentioned in both, but such vows are customary between
husband and wife.   The husband is described as an exile as a
result of a feud in HM (19-20), and the husband in WL may
have left hurriedly as a result of a crime (6-7, 18-21).   The
theme of exile is, however, a stock one in elegiac poems, as,
for example, in *The Wanderer* and *The Seafarer* ; in poems on
the theme of separation its occurrence is hardly surprising.
The woman has enemies in WL (11-14), and in HM (24-5) the
injunction to the prince's daughter to let no man hinder her
may imply that possibility, although it may also imply that
the husband has reason to believe that she will be reluctant to
obey his summons because she has been deserted by him.
Verbal echoes in both poems have been brought forward as
evidence of common origin, but these are not distinctive, in
that they can readily be traced to similarities of theme, not
necessarily of plot.   Recent investigations of the Old English
poetic vocabulary have shown the extent to which it is stereo-
typed and how little reliance can be placed on verbal parallels
as indications of common authorship.[2]

[1] Originated by Grein, *Kurzgefasste angelsächsische Grammatik*
(Kassel, 1880), p. 10, but most fully expounded by Trautmann, *loc. cit.*
pp. 222-5.
[2] Cf. especially F. P. Magoun (Jr.), ' Oral-Formulaic Character
of Anglo-Saxon Narrative Poetry ', *Speculum*, xxviii (1953), 446-67,

Against a relationship between the two poems is the difference in atmosphere and emphasis. The attitudes of the lovers are not complementary. In WL it is the woman who is filled with impassioned longing (7-8, 13-14, 32-3, 52-3) ; in HM it is the man who desires that his consort shall come and share his newly-won fortune with him (27-9, 44-8). Even when allowance has been made for the fact that we look through the eyes alternately of the woman and the man, it remains true that in HM the whole poem aims at convincing the woman of the man's fidelity, presupposes that his departure may have given her cause for disillusionment with him, and hints that her obedience to the call is by no means taken for granted ; whereas in WL there is no doubt about the woman's desire to be with her husband. On the husband's love for the woman who utters the lament, WL is almost silent ; there is a possible hint in lines 51 f. that he will desire to be with her.

In a larger context of prose or poetry these different attitudes in the monologues could perhaps be reconciled on the basis of dramatic irony. The wife despairs of reunion with her husband because of his adverse fortunes, whereas he has in fact prospered. He on his part doubts whether her love for him has stood the strain of his involuntary desertion of her, whereas it has in reality made her passion for him stronger than ever. A supposition of this kind, however, requires us to supply much of the plot, without explicit justification from the texts. We are given clearly-defined but meagre situations, with just sufficient solid basis to give credibility to the sentiments which are the main business of these poems, variations on the same basic human themes of separation and love-longing. There are loose ends in both, like the role of the husband's kin in WL (11-14) and the journey southwards which the woman is urged to undertake in HM (26-8), and their presence suggests wider and perhaps less elevated contexts, in verse or perhaps prose, from which these self-contained lyrics have been abstracted. But the setting of one may well have been quite unrelated to that of the other, if such settings ever existed.

S. B. Greenfield, ' The Formulaic Expression of the Theme of " Exile " in Anglo-Saxon Poetry ', *Speculum*, xxx (1955), 200-6, and L. J. Peters, ' The Relationship of the Old English *Andreas* to *Beowulf* ', *PMLA*, lxvi (1951), 844-63.

Apart from Imelmann's Odoaker saga, discussed above, the only external source put forward for *The Husband's Message* is a tale which became absorbed into the Tristram cycle.[1] Tristram returns secretly from exile and hides in the forest near Ysolt's home. He carves a message on a piece of wood and leaves it in the road along which she will pass. In the message he declares that he cannot live without her, that it is with them as with the honeysuckle and the hazel, which, once intertwined, cannot be separated without the destruction of both. But this image, central to the tale, cannot be found in the runes or in the text of our poem, which has, moreover, no recognisable affinity with the tale unless it be assumed that the rune-stave itself in *The Husband's Message* contains the substance of the poem.

The Poem

The anguish of *The Wife's Lament* is absent here, for the initiative is in the hands of the husband, the originator of the message. The period of separation has been involuntary, but he can decide when to terminate it. The fierce passion of the first poem is also absent, for love-longing is not the only consideration ; the possession of wealth and power has had to be a prelude to reunion. The man's wife is to set the seal on his achievements, to make them all worth the winning.

The tone is aristocratic. The man's very real desire for the woman is controlled and set against an exalted social background. His vision of their life together has a social setting. He sees himself and her in the role of lord and lady, dispensing treasure to their retainers. The key word here is *genōh* (35) ; he has enough of the wealth which their position in society demands, to justify him in sending for her now.

There is a formality about the message which is largely the result of its transmission by a third person, the messenger, who, after introducing himself in lines 1-12, becomes merely the mouthpiece of the absent husband in lines 13-25, the reporter of his words, referring to his lord's commands in lines 13 and 20 f. as the authority for his statements. This passage is clearly marked off from the introductory matter

---

[1] W. H. Schofield, *English Literature from the Norman Conquest to Chaucer* (London, 1906), pp. 201-2.

by the beginning of a new section at line 13, and from what
follows, by a sectional division after line 25. The opening
lines of the next passage contain the messenger's own advice
to the woman. Roeder would include lines 24 and 25 here ;
but these belong with the message proper, because of the
intensely personal note, which is out of keeping with the
messenger, and because of the continued absence of any
references to the husband, such as occur in every sentence
from line 26 onwards. The exhortations in lines 26 and 27
have the appearance of spontaneous advice, for the subor-
dinate clause with *monnan* and *þēoden þin*, in the following
lines, shows that the messenger is talking to the woman about
her husband, and no longer delivering a set message. The
husband has asked her to set out when she hears the cuckoo
(21-3). Its song was traditionally the herald of fair weather.[1]
Good sailing weather must have brought the messenger
himself, hence his injunction to her to set out immediately.
Throughout the rest of the passage the messenger's many
indirect references to the husband show him choosing his own
way of informing her about her husband's fortunes and aspira-
tions in his adopted country overseas.

The restrained atmosphere is not entirely due to the inter-
posal of a messenger. There is a certain anxiety lest his wife
should not come. Twice, in identical terms, there is an appeal
to the vows they made in days gone by. The desolate state
in which he went into exile is contrasted with his achievements
since, as if to enhance their magnitude and raise him in her
eyes. The worthlessness of worldly possessions to him, if she
is not there to share them, is emphasised. The reference to
the sad song of the cuckoo, with its overtones of the melan-
choly of separation, the exhortation to let no man hinder her
departure, are also signs of anxiety. There is throughout a
deference which indicates that her compliance is not taken
for granted.

The elegiac note here is not fierce and turbulent as in *The
Wife's Lament*, but gentle and melancholy, evoking the future
that opens up before them in terms of the past. The more
formal and restrained atmosphere of the poem is reflected in
the careful choice of vocabulary. This is occasionally merely

[1] See E. A. Armstrong, *The Folklore of Birds* (London, 1958), pp.
197-200.

ornate, as *on gewitlocan* (15) and *faran on flotweg . . . mengan*
merestrēamas (42-3), but there are other words and phrases
which appear to be chosen more purposefully, for their state-
liness as well as their significance, such as *tīrfæste trēowe* (12),
sinchroden (14), *sigepēode* (20). Some compound words and
phrases have a repetitive element in them which adds little of
vividness or significance to them, as *mōdlufan* (10), *wordbēotunga*
(15), *sǣnacan* (27), *on hyge hycge* (11), *eard weardigan, ān lond*
būgan (18), *sipes getwǣfan, lāde gelettan* (24-5). The function
of these appears to be to slow down the verse and emphasise
vital points in the message. Even the simpler passages
contain carefully balanced parentheses, without the terse
headlong effect of so much of *The Wife's Lament*, so that the
result is a calculated precision of utterance, an appeal which
is sincere, but nevertheless intentionally moving, and above
all, sophisticated.

THE RUIN

Unlike the two poems already discussed, *The Ruin* is
impersonal and contemplative. The poet describes a place
in ruins and muses on the fate and fortunes of its former
inhabitants. The main point at issue is whether he is depict-
ing one particular site which he has seen, or whether he is
presenting a generalised composite picture of a number of
ruins, as is held by Krapp-Dobbie.[1] The stone ruins are
described in many passages in such detail as to give the
impression that the poem is an eye-witness account of a visible
remnant of Roman civilisation in Anglo-Saxon England. The
references to baths and thermal springs in particular have led
to the claim that the site is Bath.[2] The hot springs there were
celebrated in Anglo-Saxon times, but the only evidence for a
knowledge of the existence of the baths is embodied in the
city's Anglo-Saxon names : *Hat Bathu* and similar forms,[3]

---

[1] *op. cit.* p. lxv.

[2] H. Leo, *Carmen Anglo-Saxonicum in Codice Exoniensi servatum,*
quod vulgo inscribitur ' Ruinae ' (Halle, 1865), and J. Earle, ' An
Ancient Saxon Poem of a City in Ruins, supposed to be Bath ', *Pro-*
ceedings of the Bath Natural History and Antiquities Field Club, ii
(1870-3), 259-70 ; cf. also C. A. Hotchner, *Wessex and Old English*
Poetry, with special consideration of ' The Ruin ' (New York, 1939).

[3] J. M. Kemble, *Codex Diplomaticus Aevi Saxonici*, 6 vols. (London,
1839-48), nos. 12, 290, 566.

and *æt Baþum*.[1] From 973 onward it is known simply as *Baðan*,[2] or in Latin as *Bathonia*.[3] Clearly the designation of the city was becoming a label rather than a description of its outstanding phenomenon.

The writers of charters occasionally turn aside from their main business to describe the thermal springs.[4] The biographer of St. Dunstan, writing at the beginning of the eleventh century, refers to Bath as a place where hot springs burst forth from their hiding place in the abyss in steaming droplets, a place which the inhabitants call *Bathum* in the vernacular.[5] This is a description comparable with that in lines 38-41 of *The Ruin*. The main difference lies in the greater detail of the poet. He shows an awareness of the reservoir built to contain the waters of the springs and also of the means by which the waters were distributed.

The poet makes many references to the architecture of the city, and his descriptions of stone walls, tiles, towers, arched roofs and foundations bonded with metal establish that the ruined buildings are of Roman construction. Much of the description could, nevertheless, be applied to many Roman works all over the country. There are, however, three features which, taken in conjunction, fit Bath but no other known site in Britain ; and there are several others which are not easily explicable except in terms of that locality.

One distinctive feature is the hot spring rising into a walled reservoir (38b-41a). It has been contended that the passage could quite as well contain a reference to water heated by hypocausts as to thermal springs.[6] The poet, however, states that the baths were *hāt on hreþre* (41a), a phrase which, as shown in the Notes, is used only with reference to self-generated heat in Old English. The poet states : *strēam hāte wearp widan wylme* (38b-39a). It was the Roman practice

---

[1] W. de G. Birch, *Cartularium Saxonicum*, 3 vols. (London, 1885-93), nos. 241, 277, 327.

[2] *The Anglo-Saxon Chronicle*, s.a. 973.

[3] Kemble, *op. cit.* nos. 585, 593, 643.

[4] Kemble, *op. cit.* nos. 440, 585.

[5] W. Stubbs, *Memorials of St. Dunstan*, Rolls Series 52 (London, 1870), p. 46.

[6] S. J. Herben, ' *The Ruin* ', *MLN*, liv (1939), 37-9, and G. W. Dunleavy, ' A " De Excidio " Tradition in the Old English *Ruin* ', *PQ*, xxxviii (1959), 115-17.

to build baths at a low level to avoid expensive pumping arrangements. The flow of water under the action of gravity is not powerful enough to justify the use of the verb *weorpan*, ' to throw ', which is much more appropriate to a spring. There is reason to believe that the springs at Bath were as powerful in the Anglo-Saxon period as they are today, because of the degree to which their action silted up the Roman remains, and the much higher level at which they forced their way to the surface in medieval times. As for the use of *hāte*, the thermal springs at Bath alone are of a temperature sufficiently high, more than 104°F. nowadays, to justify this adverb ; that conditions were similar in Anglo-Saxon times appears to be borne out by the use of a descriptive phrase with the adjective *hāt*, namely *æt þǣm hātum baðum*,[1] as a designation for Bath. The poet goes on to say that a wall completely enclosed the gushing stream (39b-40). The main spring at Bath is situated under the modern King's Bath, and excavation has revealed that the Romans built an irregular octagonal wall round the spring to act as a reservoir for the waters, a wall of masonry three feet thick and six feet high, giving a pool with a diameter of fifty feet.

Another distinctive feature is the extent and number of the baths as indicated by *burnsele monige* (21b). In the third century Solinus described the hot springs at Bath as luxuriously furnished for human use.[2] Although the city was probably not large, the public buildings and baths were on a splendid scale. A suite of baths, lying south of the present Pump Room and Abbey churchyard, stretched at least a hundred yards from east to west and sixty yards from north to south.

A third distinctive feature is the *hringmere*, the circular pool of line 45. From the remains of the last eight lines of the poem (42-9), it is evident that the poet is describing the way in which he believed the water in the reservoir was distributed to where it was required. Many of the Roman conduits, lined with lead, are visible at the present day ; they led the water to the series of shallower rectangular and cir-

---

[1] Kemble, *op. cit.* no. 290.

[2] F. Haverfield, ' Romano-British Somerset ', *The Victoria County History of Somerset*, i (London, 1906), p. 221, and Mommsen's edition of Solinus, *Collectanea rerum memorabilium*, 1895, p. 102.

cular pools which are to be seen today. The poet says :
*lēton ponne gēotan . . . ofer hārne stān, hāte strēamas . . . oþ
þæt hringmere* (42-5). To the west of the large rectangular
Great Bath lies a circular bath, largest of all the lesser baths
in the range.

There are other references which support the claim of Bath
to be the site of the poem. In line 10 the poet describes a
wall as *ræghār ond rēadfāh*, ' grey with lichen and stained with
red '. The oolite of which the buildings are constructed has,
in addition to the more usual grey varieties of lichen, one
which covers walls with a film of orange-tinted growth, and
which provides an explanation of *rēadfāh* in this context.
The reddish lichen is *fāh*, or variegated with, the grey. Lines
30-1 appear to refer to the inside of a curved roof, ceiled with
red tiles, as indicated by the linguistic analysis of this difficult
passage in the Notes. The Great Bath at Bath was found on
excavation to be filled with the debris of tiled roofage. A
tunnel or barrel vault, made of hollow box tiles, had been put
over the bath at a date later than the original construction of
the baths.[1] The poem appears to tell how the red vault, the
ceiling of the curved inner roofwork, has parted from its tiles.
The box tiles of barrel vaults were rendered with concrete,
usually whitish, but containing a good deal of broken tile
aggregate.[2] The meticulous description of the poem accords
well with peeling off from the box tiles of such concrete. In
lines 19-20 the poet states that a skilled man bound the wall
foundations wondrously together ' with wires ', *wīrum*, into
rings or circles. Mr. S. J. Herben cites this passage in support
of his belief that Hadrian's Wall is the site of the poem, and
claims that it refers to the method of binding the stones of
circular bridge piers together, as at the Roman bridge near
Chollerford,[3] an example of this type of construction already
pointed out by Miss Kershaw. But there is no mention of a
bridge in the poem and, since in Roman construction it was
customary for large blocks of stone to be held together by iron

[1] The revised edition of the official handbook of the Corporation of
Bath, *The Roman Baths of Bath*, by R. E. M. Wheeler and B. H. St. J.
O'Neil (Bath, 1954), pp. 14-18.

[2] From information supplied by Professor I. A. Richmond in corres-
pondence with the editor in September 1957, from which Professor
Richmond has kindly permitted him to quote.

[3] *MLN*, liv. 37-9.

cramps, the reference would be quite as applicable to the
foundations of large columns such as those which supported
the Great Bath roof. Professor Richmond has found in his
excavations at Bath abundant evidence in the stonework for
the use of cramps in the baths.

In his articles Herben has justly refuted claims made for
Bath by Miss Hotchner in respect of architectural features
and materials which are widely distributed among Roman
remains, but he fails to shake the evidence for Bath of the
detailed descriptions of the baths and hot springs. Moreover,
he concludes his second article with an assumption that the
poet was writing in Northumbria : ' I cannot feel otherwise
than that the poet was writing about the nearer, and infinitely
more impressive ruin ',[1] namely Hadrian's Wall. The
assumption of a Northumbrian origin for the poem implicit
in the word ' nearer ' is one for which he brings forward no
linguistic or other evidence. There is no trace of any dis-
tinctively Northumbrian form in the whole poem.

There remains the question as to when the ruins could
have been observed in the state described by the poet. A
local archaeologist noted in 1869 that the extensive founda-
tions of the Roman buildings were covered by mud, vegetable
remains and driftwood, the deposit in some instances being
almost converted to peat.[2] The baths disappeared because
they had been constructed below the natural surface in order
to enjoy a fuller inflow. Their walls and roofs fell in and the
hot springs, still forcing their way upwards, formed new pools
at a higher level. Haverfield describes the discovery of a
tenth-century cemetery above the eastern part of the baths.[3]
One coffin lay nearly level with the floor of a hypocaust room
and another was set on the broken shaft of a pilaster. He
concludes that after five centuries of silting up, all traces of
the Roman baths had disappeared. The location of the
coffins suggests that the surface in the tenth century was some
eight feet above the level of the Roman floors of the baths.
It follows from the poet's references to baths (lines 21, 40, 46),
that siltation could not have proceeded very far, otherwise
they would not have been visible to him.

[1] ' The Ruin Again ', MLN, lix (1944), 72-4.
[2] C. Moore, Proceedings of the Bath Natural History and Antiquities
Field Club, ii. 42.   [3] loc. cit. pp. 224-5.

A century or two must be allowed for silting up and the
falling of debris (referred to in lines 31-2) to raise the level
of the site to the height indicated for the middle of the tenth
century by the finding of the coffins and of the sepulchral
cross of *Eadgifu*, sister of a convent.[1] Further information
about Bath is to be found in the early ninth-century *Historia
Brittonum* by Nennius, in the appendix dealing with the
wonders of Britain. The third wonder is a hot pool in the
territory of the Hwicce ; the pool is surrounded by a wall
made of brick and stone, and when one enters it at any time
to bathe the water will be hot or cold according to one's
desire.[2] Nennius cannot be referring to the Roman baths,
for these were sunk in the floor. The reference to the wall
recalls lines 39-40 of *The Ruin* and the Roman reservoir
discussed above. It would be perilous to assume from Nen-
nius's concentration on the walled pool that no other structures
were still standing, but from his reference to the fluctuation
in temperature of the water it can be inferred that the level of
the surrounding marshy land was not far below that of the
reservoir top. Professor Richmond has noted that flooding
of the area was due not only to the springs but to the waters
of the Avon. Even today, with the Roman drains and sluices
reopened, extensive flooding occasionally takes place. The
reservoir naturally stood at the highest point in order that
gravity should supply the water to the baths. The ground
level must have risen considerably beyond the Roman floor
level to have permitted river water to back up the outlets
from the reservoir and dilute the water there. The obvious
extravagance of Nennius's claim that the water could be made
hot or cold at will should not blind us to the phenomenon
which could give rise to the idea. The water would be hot
when composed of spring water alone ; it would be tepid or
cold when Avon water was added, by a rise in the level of the
river, to that of the thermal springs welling up in the reservoir.
Allowing for an interval during which the lower levels of the
baths were obliterated by siltation to the time at the beginning
of the ninth century when Nennius made his observations, it
may be said with some probability that *The Ruin* describes

---

[1] *The Roman Baths of Bath*, p. 24.
[2] F. Lot, *Nennius et l'Historia Brittonum* (Paris, 1934), p. 212.

the scene as it must have appeared no later than the first half
of the eighth century.

THE POEM

The most striking characteristic of the poet is his gift of
vivid description. He maintains variety by his ability to
alternate a sweeping panoramic view with a sharp focusing
on significant detail, as in lines 3-4 and 29-31, so that the effect
is of a vast desolation, intensified here and there by the pathos
of the decay of individually portrayed objects. These are
picked out by the use of the demonstrative adjective *þæs* and
are presented with a clarity and concrete detail which carry
the conviction that they are the fruit of personal observation.

The poet devotes the first six lines to a description of the
ruins from a general point of view, as they would appear to
one viewing the scene as a whole. With line 6b he transfers
his interest from the buildings to the builders, long dead,
immobile in the earth ; they appear to be awaiting the end of
the world, for a hundred generations (line 8) can imply little
else to the medieval mind, with its expectation of the passing
away of this world within a finite period of time. This wall
by which he stands has outlived them all ; he has come back
to the ruins themselves (line 9b). Alternation between the
works of men and those who built them or dwelt in them, as
well as alternation between past and present, is the means by
which the poet evokes warmth and poignancy in a poem whose
central theme is the atmosphere of place. From lines 12-18
the text is unfortunately in a fragmentary state ; but the
poet appears to have been dealing with the antiquity of the
ruins and the skill required to construct the buildings now in
decay, the theme with which he also closes this passage,
lines 18-20.

With line 21 he reverts to the past once more, to the age
when all these buildings were intact in their splendour and
those who occupied them at the zenith of their glory. Sud-
denly and dramatically the tone changes. Fate has reversed
her favours, death stalks among the inhabitants, and all are
carried off. Desolate, untended, the buildings moulder. A
passage similar in outlook to this occurs in *Beowulf* 2255-60,

where the last survivor of his race laments the decay that will overtake his treasure and arms. It may be noted that two of the conventional agents of death of the Anglo-Saxon poets, *ādl*, *yldo* and *ecg*, are absent. Pestilence alone is mentioned by the poet and held to be responsible for the ruinous state of the buildings. There is no indication of a city destroyed by fire and sword as has often been said of *The Ruin* ; on the contrary, it is the obvious appearance of decay, not destruction, which is the keynote of the poem and which leads the writer to suppose that some disease overwhelmed the inhabitants.

From line 18, and perhaps before, the poet has been wandering among the ruins, recording what he saw as he went. In line 30 he pauses to look up at one of the most striking of the remains. Its grandeur evokes in his mind the way of life of those who lived there. He indulges in an imaginative reconstruction of their wealth and luxury (lines 32b-37), viewing the scene through their eyes. But the colours of his imagination are entirely Germanic ; his picture is that of the Germanic warrior of the Heroic Age, adorned with gold (33), proud and flushed with wine in his bright armour (34) ; the language can be paralleled from many a similar description in *Beowulf* and elsewhere. Here, as in other parts of the poem, there is a powerful contrast between the sharply defined ruins and the vaguely though sympathetically imagined inhabitants.

So far the style has been formal and exalted ; but a change comes over it at line 38. The poet has come upon the baths. Hitherto the scene was strange, though capable of being translated into the terms of the life he knew ; but here is something beyond his experience. He displays astonishment, almost the innocent wonder and delight of a child. His style becomes straightforwardly descriptive, unadorned with variant compounds and elaborate epithets. He becomes almost incoherent in places and repeats himself wholly or in part in the same words in lines 40b and 46b, in 38b, 43b and possibly 45b, and in 41b and 48b. The last few lines are mutilated and fragmentary, but it is on a note of awe and approval that the poem closes. Both the balanced structure of the poem and the poet's technique in repeatedly narrowing and sharpening the focus of attention give support to the belief that he has in mind a single site and not a composite picture of many ruins.

Similarities between *The Ruin* and other Old English poems have often been pointed out. These are particularly striking between *The Wanderer*, 76b-77a, 78a, 78b-79a, 79b-80a, 87, 88a, 100b and *The Ruin*, lines 3a and 4b, 12, 6b-7b, 28b-29a, 2b, 1a and 28b, 24b. They are, however, not close enough to require the supposition that one poet influenced the other, but are explicable on the grounds of the similarity of subject matter of the impersonal elegiac passages of *The Wanderer* and most of *The Ruin*. The writer of *The Wanderer*, moreover, has a purpose different from that of the author of *The Ruin* ; he uses scenes of decay to point a moral, whereas the tone of our poet is detached and disinterested. Nevertheless, the similarity of theme, of vocabulary and of technique, especially the technique of alternation—between past and present, the general and the particular, men and their works—lends colour to the belief that the two poems belong to a common tradition of poetic composition.

The Cynewulfian elegiac passage near the end of *Christ* II has affinities in vocabulary and outlook with *The Ruin*, especially lines 810-14, which recall the opening passage of our poem, echoing its wording in *burgstede berstað* (811). Similar close parallels in phraseology have been pointed out by Miss Hotchner between some of the gnomic verses (*Maxims* II) and our poem ; [1] cf. *orðanc enta geweorc* (2a) and *wrætlic weallstāna geweorc* (3a) in the former with lines 2b and 1a in *The Ruin*.

Conybeare pointed out the similarity in theme to Llywarch Hen's early Welsh elegy on Urien Rheged. [2] There too the poet surveys a ruined city, Shrewsbury, and points the contrast between its present desolation and the joy and grandeur it knew when inhabited. It is a strange historical link with Bath that the West-Saxon army which gained the city by the Battle of Deorham, was the same which pushed on up the Severn valley to defeat the Celts at Shrewsbury, and thus gave occasion for this Celtic elegy.

---

[1] *op. cit.* p. 89.
[2] J. J. and W. D. Conybeare, *Illustrations of Anglo-Saxon Poetry* (London, 1826), pp. 250-1.

DIALECT

These poems, like most others that have survived from the Old English period, are written in the late West Saxon dialect contemporary or nearly contemporary with the period of the MS. in which they are preserved. Here and there occur linguistic forms foreign to this dialect ; these are generally presumed to have survived from an earlier stage of their transmission, perhaps from the dialects of the poets. The confident assumption that much of the earlier poetry, including these poems, is of non-West-Saxon origin has been seriously undermined. As Dr. Sisam has reminded us, 'poems could be produced that do not belong to any local dialect, but to a general Old English poetic dialect, artificial, archaic, and perhaps mixed in its vocabulary, conservative in inflexions that affect the verse-structure, and indifferent to non-structural irregularities, which were perhaps tolerated as part of the colouring of the language of verse'.[1]

Features which are held to be of non-West-Saxon origin are as follows :

1. Non-West-Saxon *ē* in place of WS *ǣ* (from Gmc *ǣ*) is found in *brērum* WL 31, *hwætrēd* R 19, *fēlon* R 13 ; *ǣ* occurs nine times in WL, thirteen in HM and five in R.

2. *a* before *ld* instead of the fractured *ea* usual in WS may be Anglian [Sievers-Brunner, § 85 and Anm. 1] and appears in *alwaldend* HM 32, *waldendwyrhtan* R 7 ; in *ældo* R 6, earlier *a* has undergone *i*-mutation. These forms are, however, widespread in OE and may have been common poetic forms.

3. Back mutation of *e* to *eo* before *d* or *t* is rare outside Anglian [Sievers-Brunner, § 110, Anm. 1]. It occurs in *meoduburgum* HM 17, *meododrēama* HM 46, *meodoheall* R 23, and also in *undereotone* R 6, which can be paralleled with *eo* in other forms of the verb *etan* only in Mercian texts, and most frequently in the *Vespasian Psalter* (see Note to R 6).

4. Back mutation of *æ* to *ea* is seen in *geador* HM 29 (cf. *togædre* R 20), and is held to be Mercian, but this word may

[1] K. Sisam, 'Dialect Origins of the Earlier Old English Verse', *Studies in the History of Old English Literature* (Oxford, 1953), p. 138 ; cf. also A. Campbell, *Old English Grammar* (Oxford, 1959), pp. 9-10.

well have been in general poetic use. [Sievers-Brunner, § 109, Ann. 3.]

5. Lack of syncope of the vowel in the inflexions of the 2nd and 3rd singular present indicative of verbs is held to be an Anglian feature [Johannes Hedberg, *The Syncope of the Old English Present Endings*, Lund, 1945], although such forms may have had wide currency in other Old English dialects up to and including the time of Alfred [Hedberg, p. 286, Sisam, pp. 123-5]. Unsyncopated forms which have no umlaut of the stem vowel are regarded as purely Anglian [Hedberg, p. 287] ; examples are *drēogeð* WL 50 and *sceādeð* R 30. Other unsyncopated forms are *siteð* WL 47 and *findest* HM 12, 28. Syncopated forms do not occur in any of the poems. In all the examples except that in WL 50 the unsyncopated form is essential to the metre.

6. The preterite ending *-ade* and the pp. ending *-ad* are the rule in Anglian in Class 2 weak verbs in contrast to *-ode* and *-od* in WS ; *-ede* and *-ed* are rare but occur in all dialects [Sievers-Brunner, §§ 413, 414]. Forms with *a* and *e* are found in all three texts : *longade* WL 14, *oflongad* WL 29, *brosnade* R 28, *bēotedan* WL 21, *næglede* HM 35, *gefrætwed* R 33. No forms with *o* occur. Past participles and preterites with both *a* and *e*, but not *o*, are most frequent in the *Vespasian Psalter* [Sievers-Brunner, § 413, Anm. 6, § 414, Anm. 4].

7. The retention of *g* before *d* is regular in Anglian, but may have been a common archaism in poetry [Sievers-Brunner, §. 389, 2, Anm. 1]. Examples are *sægde* HM 31, *gebrægd*, R 18.

8. In the Mercian and South Northumbrian Glosses, Class 2 weak verbs have often *-igan* instead of *-ian* as in *weardigan* HM 18 [Sievers-Brunner, § 412, Anm. 9] ; cf. *wunian* WL 27 and *weardiað* WL 34.

9. Anglian, but perhaps a common poetic form also, is *heht* in place of WS *hēt*. [Sievers-Brunner, § 394, 1.] Both forms occur, *heht* in WL 27, HM 20 and *hēt* in WL 15, HM 13.

10. The form *tigelum* R 30, with retention of intervocalic *g* and lack of syncope of the *e*, is probably Mercian, with weakening of the earlier *u* to *e* ; cf. *Vespasian Psalter*, *tigule* and Corpus Glossary *tigilum* [Sievers-Brunner, § 159, Anm. 3 and 4].

11. Non-West-Saxon are the forms *lifgende* WL **34**, *lifgendne* HM 25, *lifgendum* HM 53 [Sievers-Brunner, § 417, Anm. 2(*d*)].

12. The genitive plural form *cnēa* R 8 has only one parallel, the similar form *trēa* in the *Vespasian Psalter*, 73.5. [See Sievers-Brunner, § 250, Anm. 4 and cf. Campbell, § 278(*b*) and 279.]

13. The form *þæs* (R 9, 30) is Anglian [Sievers-Brunner, § 338, Anm. 4] ; cf. the WS form *þes* in WL 29. In R 1 *þes* appears to be an alteration from *þæs* (see Notes).

14. The combination of *ūp* as an adverb with a verb [*ā*]*wēox* or *wēox*, as in WL 3, is a syntactical feature found only in Mercian documents.[1]

15. Words with forms or meanings generally held to be Anglian[2] occur in all three poems : *wrecan* meaning ' to utter ', WL 1 (J. J. Campbell, p. 366), *morþor* WL 20 (Jordan, p. 106), *nemne* WL 22 for WS *nefne* (J. J. Campbell, p. 262, Jordan, pp. 46-8), *þenden* HM 17 (J. J. Campbell, p. 365), *geleorene* R 7 (J. J. Campbell, p. 361, Jordan, pp. 44-6).

All three poems are seen to possess distinctively Anglian features in phonology or vocabulary, even when allowance is made for features which may point to an earlier general poetic tradition. The number and diversity of Anglian forms in these poems make it unlikely that they are all to be explained as exceptional usages within West Saxon. Moreover, among the unusually large proportions of unique or rare words in *The Ruin*, it is precisely those words such as *hwætrēd* R 19 and *forweorone* R 7 (which do not occur elsewhere), and *geleorene* R 7 (which is rare, and unknown outside Anglian), which display unmistakably Anglian features ; unrecognised by a West Saxon, it is reasonable to assume that they would be transcribed unaltered.

Although it cannot be said with any certainty where in the Anglian area these poems were written, their affinities are with Mercian rather than Northumbrian. *The Ruin* in particular has features in common with the *Vespasian Psalter*

---

[1] J. J. Campbell, ' The Dialect Vocabulary of the OE Bede ', *JEGP*, l (1951), 354.

[2] J. J. Campbell, *loc. cit.* pp. 361-6, and R. Jordan, *Eigentümlichkeiten des anglischen Wortschatzes* (Heidelberg, 1906).

and may well be West Mercian.[1] Since the poem describes the Roman baths at Bath, a location of the poet in or near that city would harmonise with the linguistic evidence, for within the probable period of composition of the poem Bath was part of Mercian territory. The use of Celtic literary motifs, closely paralleled in early Welsh literature in both *The Wife's Lament* and *The Husband's Message* (see pp. 11 and 61) suggests that a Mercian setting for these also would harmonise with such linguistic indications of dialect as there are.

DATE

Many of the metrical and linguistic criteria formerly used to establish the approximate date of composition of an Old English poem have been shown to be unreliable,[2] but some are still useful provided that the findings are not too narrowly interpreted and that sufficient allowance is made for the preservation of archaic forms in poetic diction.[3]

Of Morsbach's linguistic tests,[4] the only one which can be unambiguously applied concerns the treatment by the poet of contracted forms resulting from the loss of an intervocalic consonant. Originally disyllabic forms became monosyllabic when the vowels combined to form diphthongs. It is generally held that if the metre requires the scansion of such a form as disyllabic, then the line was composed at a period not long after the disappearance of the intervocalic consonant, i.e. early in the eighth century.[5] There is one example in each of the three poems : *fromsiþ frēan* WL 33, *mines frēan* HM 10, and *oþ hund cnēa* R 8. To make any metrical pattern, each of these contracted forms requires to be read as disyllabic.

---

[1] R. M. Wilson has, however, shown that a Mercian provenance for the *Vespasian Psalter* glosses is by no means certain; *v.* ' The Provenance of the Vespasian Psalter: The Linguistic Evidence ', in *The Anglo-Saxons, Studies in some Aspects of their History and Culture*, presented to Bruce Dickins (London, 1959), pp. 280-310.

[2] D. Whitelock, ' Anglo-Saxon Poetry and the Historian ', *Trans. of the Royal Historical Society*, xxxi (1949), 75-94, and *The Audience of Beowulf* (Oxford, 1951).

[3] C. L. Wrenn, *Beowulf* (London, 1953), pp. 32-4.

[4] *Zur Datierung des Beowulfes* (Göttingen, 1906).

[5] R. Girvan, *Beowulf and the 7th Century* (London, 1935), p. 20.

Another linguistic and metrical test is for the presence or absence before liquids or nasals of inorganic vowels, held to have been introduced early in the eighth century.[1] There is only one example which can be tested by the metre, *morþor hycgendne* WL 20 ; here the metrical pattern may be improved if *morþor* is taken as a monosyllable.

Lichtenheld's syntactical tests for an early date [2] rest on the deduction that at an early period the construction weak adjective plus noun was predominant, whereas later the weak adjective is found only after the definite article. There are five examples from all three poems of the former construction : *wynlicran wīc* WL 52, *fǣdan goldes* HM 36, *brādan rīces* R 37, *wīdan wylme* R 39, *beorhtan bōsme* R 40, but none with the latter construction ; two phrases, *wyrd sēo swīþe* R 24, because of the word order, and *þās beorhtan burg* R 37, because of the use of the compound demonstrative, are outside the scope of the construction we are considering, for the demonstrative is emphasised. Lichtenheld also observed that the use of the weak adjective with the instrumental case of nouns was one which rapidly diminished ; examples occur in R 39 and 40 cited above.

Such linguistic and metrical evidence as there is would appear to support the usual attribution of these poems to the eighth century. The flexibility of the syntax, the thorough integration of kennings into the flow of the verse without impeding its movement, the expert handling of the alliterative verse technique to effect changes of pace and mood, these are features which suggest a period prior to the more ornate and elaborate verse of the Cynewulfian school. All three poems contain words, and compounds in particular, which do not occur elsewhere ; some, such as *tēaforgēapa* R 30, may describe unique features, but most cannot be explained in this way. Others may, of course, have been used at a later period, in literature which has not survived. Nevertheless, the proportion of unusual words is so high that it is difficult to avoid the conclusion that some were to become obsolete later in the

[1] Sievers-Brunner, § § 152, 153.
[2] ' Das schwache Adjectiv im Angelsächsischen ', *ZfdA*, xvi (1873), 325-93. See also A. J. Barnouw, *Textkritische Untersuchungen nach dem Gebrauch des bestimmten Artikels und des schwachen Adjectivs in der altenglischen Poesie* (Leiden, 1902).

Old English period, and that they appear in these poems because they were written before the alliterative tradition hardened. *The Ruin* on all counts appears to be the earliest of the three. There is some contextual evidence (pp. 26-28) pointing to a date of composition before the middle of the eighth century, if it is accepted that the subject of the poem is Bath. Linguistic evidence for date and place is far from decisive, but what there is agrees with that derived from the context of the poem.

SELECT BIBLIOGRAPHY

Editions are listed chronologically, other works in alphabetical order within each section.

MANUSCRIPT AND FACSIMILES

CHAMBERS, R. W. 'The British Museum Transcript of the Exeter Book (Add. MS. 9067)', *Anglia*, xxxv (1911-12), 393-400.

HOLTHAUSEN, F. 'Zur altenglischen literatur, XIII', *Anglia Beiblatt*, xxiii (1912), 83-7.

KER, N. R. *Catalogue of Manuscripts containing Anglo-Saxon.* Oxford, 1957.

SISAM. K. 'The Exeter Book', *Studies in the History of Old English Literature.* Oxford, 1953, pp. 97-108.

The Exeter Book of Old English Poetry. London, 1933. Collotype facsimile edition, with introductory chapters by R. W. CHAMBERS, MAX FÖRSTER, and ROBIN FLOWER.

Transcript of the *Exeter Book*, British Museum Additional MS. 9067, collated with the original by Sir Frederic Madden in 1832.

TUPPER, FR. (Jr.). 'The British Museum Transcript of the Exeter Book (Add. MS. 9067)', *Anglia*, xxxvi (1912), 285-8.

EDITIONS

Where an edition does not contain all three poems, those included are given in square brackets after an entry.

CONYBEARE, J. J. and W. D. *Illustrations of Anglo-Saxon Poetry.* London, 1826. [WL, R]

CRAIGIE, W. A. *Specimens of Anglo-Saxon Poetry, III. Germanic Legend and Anglo-Saxon History and Life.* Edinburgh, 1931.

EARLE, J. 'The Ruined City', *Academy*, xxvi (1884), 29. [R]

ETTMÜLLER, L. *Engla and Seaxna Scôpas and Bôceras.* Quedlinburg and Leipzig, 1850.

GREIN, C. W. M. *Bibliothek der Angelsächsischen Poesie*, I. Göttingen, 1857.

GREIN, C. W. M. and WÜLKER, R. P. *Bibliothek der Angelsächsischen Poesie*, I. Kassel, 1883.

KAISER, R. *Alt- und mittelenglische Anthologie.* Third edition. Berlin, 1958.

KERSHAW, N. *Anglo-Saxon and Norse Poems.* Cambridge, 1922.

KLIPSTEIN, L. F. *Analecta Anglo-Saxonica*, vol. II. New York, 1849.

KLUGE, F. *Angelsächsiches Lesebuch.* Third edition. Halle, 1902.

KRAPP, G. P. and DOBBIE, E. V. K. *The Exeter Book.* The Anglo-Saxon Poetic Records, III. New York, 1936.

LEHNERT, M. *Poetry and Prose of the Anglo-Saxons.* Berlin, 1955. [R]

LEO, H. *Carmen Anglo-Saxonicum in Codice Exoneniensi servatum, quod vulgo inscribitur ' Ruinae '.* Halle, 1865. [R]

MACKIE, W. S. *The Exeter Book*, Part II. Early English Text Society, Original Series, 194. London, 1934.

MOSSÉ, F. *Manuel de l'anglais du Moyen Âge des origines au XIVe siècle.* I : Vieil-Anglais. Second edition, Paris, 1950. [R]

RICCI, A. *L'Elegia Pagana Anglosassone.* Florence, 1923.

SCHÜCKING, L. L. *Kleines Angelsächsisches Dichterbuch.* Second edition. Leipzig, 1933.

SEDGEFIELD, W. J. *An Anglo-Saxon Verse Book.* Manchester, 1922. [WL, HM]

SIEPER, E. *Die Altenglische Elegie.* Strassburg, 1915.

THORPE, B. *Codex Exoniensis.* Published for the Society of Antiquaries. London, 1842.

TRAUTMANN, M. ' Zur Botschaft des Gemahls ', *Anglia*, xvi (1894); 207-25. [HM]

WÜLKER, R. P. *Kleinere Angelsächsische Dichtungen.* Halle, 1879.

WYATT, A. J. *An Anglo-Saxon Reader.* Cambridge, 1919. [HM]

TRANSLATIONS

ABBOTT, C. C. ' Three Old English Elegies ', *Durham University Journal*, xxxvi (1943-4), 78-9. [WL, R]

BONE, G. *Anglo-Saxon Poetry*. Oxford, 1943.

COOK, A. S. and TINKER, C. B. *Select Translations from Old English Poetry*. Third edition. Harvard, 1935.

DE BRUGGER, ILSE, M. *Las Elegias Anglo-Sajonas*. Buenos Aires, 1954. [English and Spanish]

FAUST, C. and THOMPSON, S. *Old English Poems, Translated into the Original Meter*. Chicago, 1918.

GORDON, R. K. *Anglo-Saxon Poetry*. Revised edition. London, 1954.

GREIN, C. W. M. *Dichtungen der Angelsachsen stabreimend übersetzt*. vol. ii. Göttingen, 1859. [German]

JONES, C. W. *Medieval Literature in Translation*. New York, 1950. [R. in Tinker's translation]

KENNEDY, C. W. *Old English Elegies, translated into Alliterative Verse*. Princeton, 1936.

OLIVERO, F. *Traduzione della poesia anglo-sassone, con introduzione e Note*. Bari, 1915. [WL, R] [Italian].

SPAETH, J. D. *Old English Poetry. Translation into Alliterative Verse, with Introduction and Notes*. Princeton, 1922. [HM]

See also translations in the editions by Conybeare, Earle, Kershaw, Leo [German], Mackie, Sieper [German], Thorpe.

TEXTUAL STUDIES

BLACKBURN, F. A. ' The Husband's Message and the Accompanying Riddles of the Exeter Book ', *JGP*, iii (1901), 1-13.

CRAWFORD, S. J. Review of *An Anglo-Saxon Verse Book* by W. J. Sedgefield, *MLR*, xix (1924), 105.

CROSS, J. E. ' Notes on Old English Texts ', *Neophilologus*, xxxix (1955), 204-5.

CROSS, J. E. ' On Sievers-Brunner's Interpretation of *The Ruin*, Line 7, *Forweorone Geleorene* ', *English and Germanic Studies*, vi (1957), 104-06.

DEROLEZ, R. *Runica Manuscripta*. Brugge, 1954, pp. 398-9.

DIETRICH, F. 'Die Räthsel des Exeterbuchs', *ZfdA*, xi (1859), 452-3.

ELLIOTT, R. W. V. 'The Runes in *The Husband's Message*', *JEGP*, liv (1955), 1-8.

GREENFIELD, S. B. '*The Wife's Lament* Reconsidered', *PMLA*, lxviii (1953), 907-12.

GRUBL, EMILY D. *Studien zu den angelsächsischen Elegien.* Marburg, 1948.

HERBEN, S. J. 'The Ruin', *MLN*, liv (1939), 37-9.

HERBEN, S. J. 'The Ruin Again', *MLN*, lix (1944), 72-4.

HICKETIER, F. 'Klage der Frau, Botschaft des Gemahls, und Ruine', *Anglia*, xi (1889), 363-8.

HOLTHAUSEN, F. 'Zur altenglischen literatur : IV', *Anglia Beiblatt*, xviii (1907), 207-8.

HOLTHAUSEN, F. 'Zur textkritik altenglischer dichtungen', *ES*, xxxvii (1907), 200.

HOLTHAUSEN, F. 'Zur altenglischen literatur : VII', *Anglia Beiblatt*, xix (1908), 248.

HOLTHAUSEN, F. Review of *Kleines Angelsächsisches Dichterbuch* by L. L. Schücking, *Anglia Beiblatt*, xxxii (1921), 82.

HOLTHAUSEN, F. 'Zu altenglischen Dichtungen', *Anglia Beiblatt*, xxxiv (1923), 90.

HOLTHAUSEN, F. Review of *The Exeter Book*, Part II, edited by W. S. Mackie, *Anglia Beiblatt*, xlvi (1935), 9-10.

IDELMANN, THEODORA. *Das Gefühl in den altenglischen Elegien.* Münster, 1932.

IMELMANN, R. *Forschungen zur Altenglischen Poesie.* Berlin, 1920.

KIRKLAND, J. H. 'A Passage in the Anglo-Saxon Poem *The Ruin*, Critically Discussed', *AJP*, vii (1886), 367-9.

KLAEBER, FR. 'Zu Altenglischen Dichtungen', *Archiv*, clxvii (1935), 38-40.

KOCK, E. A. 'Interpretations and Emendations of Early English Texts. VIII', *Anglia*, xlv (1921), 122-3.

KOCK, E. A. 'Interpretations and Emendations of Early English Texts : X', *Anglia*, xlvi (1922), 178-9.

LAWRENCE, W. W. 'The Banished Wife's Lament', *MP*, v (1907-8), 387-405.

MACKIE, W. S. 'Notes on Old English Poetry', *MLN*, xl (1925), 92.

MERITT, H. 'Three Studies in Old English. II : An Old English Term for Waled Ornamentation ', *AJP*, lxii (1941), 334-8.

NENNINGER, J. *Die altenglische ' Ruine ' textkritisch und literhistorisch untersucht.* Limburg, 1938.

ROEDER, F. *Die Familie bei den Angelsachsen, Erster Haupteil : Mann und Frau.* Halle, 1899.

SCHAUBERT, ELSE VON. 'Zur Erklärung Schwierigkeiten bietender altenglischer Textstellen ', *Philologica : the Malone Anniversary Studies*, pp. 31-42. Baltimore, 1949.

SCHÜCKING, L. L. 'Das Angelsächsische Gedicht von der *Klage der Frau* ', *ZfdA*, xlviii (1906), 436-49.

SCHÜCKING, L. L. *Untersuchungen zur Bedeutungslehre der angelsächsischen Dichtersprache*, pp. 55, 75, 103. Heidelberg, 1915.

SCHÜCKING, L. L. Review of *Die Altenglische Elegie* by E. Sieper, *ES*, li (1917-18), 97-115.

STEVICK, ROBERT D. 'Formal Aspects of *The Wife's Lament* ', *JEGP*, lix (1960), 21-5.

STROBL, J. 'Zur Spruchdichtung bei den Angelsachsen ', *ZfdA*, xxxi (1887), 55-6.

TIMMER, B. J. 'The Elegiac Mood in Old English Poetry ', *English Studies*, xxiv (1942), 34-6.

TUPPER, F. (Jr.) 'Originals and Analogues of the *Exeter Book Riddles* ', *MLN*, xviii (1903), 98-99.

TUPPER, F. (Jr.). *The Riddles of the Exeter Book.* Boston, 1910.

WARD, J. A. '*The Wife's Lament*: An Interpretation ', *JEGP*, lix (1960), 26-33.

WÜLKER, R. P. 'Aus Englischen Bibliotheken ', *Anglia*, ii (1879), 374-87.

WYATT, A. J. *Old English Riddles.* Boston, 1912.

SOURCES AND ANALOGUES

BRANDL, A. 'Venantius Fortunatus und die Angelsächsischen Elegien *Wanderer* und *Ruine*', *Archiv*, cxxxix (1919), 84.

BROOKE, S. A. *The History of Early English Literature.* 2 vols. London, 1892.

DUNLEAVY, G. W. ' Possible Irish Analogues for *The Wife's Lament* ', *PQ*, xxxv (1956), 208-13.

REUSCHEL, HELGA. ' Ovid und die ags. Elegien ', *Beiträge*, lxii (1938), 132-42.

RICKERT, EDITH. ' The Old English Offa Saga : II ', *MP*, ii (1904-5), 365-76.

SCHICK, J. ' Die Urquelle der Offa-Konstanze-Sage ', *Brittanica, Max Förster zum sechzigsten Geburtstage*, pp. 31-56. Leipzig, 1929.

SCHLAUCH, M. *Chaucer's Constance and Accused Queens.* New York, 1927.

SCHOFIELD, W. H. *English Literature from the Norman Conquest to Chaucer.* London, 1906.

STEFANOVÍC, S. ' Das Angelsächsische Gedicht *Die Klage der Frau* ', *Anglia*, xxxii (1909), 399-433.

WALLENSKÖLD, A. G. *Le Conte de la Femme Chaste Convoitée par son Beau-Frère.* Helsingfors, 1909.

LITERARY BACKGROUND

ANDERSON, G. K. *The Literature of the Anglo-Saxons.* Oxford, 1949.

BEISSNER, F. *Geschichte der deutschen Elegie.* Berlin, 1941.

BRANDL, A. *Geschichte der Englischen Literatur.* Strassburg, 1908.

BROOKE, S. A. *English Literature from the Beginning to the Norman Conquest.* London, 1908.

CHADWICK, H. M. and N. K. *The Growth of Literature*, vol. I. Cambridge, 1932.

JACKSON, K. H. *Studies in Early Celtic Nature Poetry.* Cambridge, 1935.

KENNEDY, C. W. *The Earliest English Poetry.* New York, 1943.

MALONE, K. ' The Old English Period (to 1100) ', *A Literary History of England*, edited by A. C. Baugh (New York, 1948), pp. 3-105.

PONS, É. *Le Thème et le Sentiment de la Nature dans la Poesie Anglo-Saxonne.* Strasbourg, 1925.

WARDALE, E. E. *Chapters on Old English Literature.* London, 1935.

WILLIAMS, BLANCHE C. *Gnomic Poetry in Anglo-Saxon*. New York, 1914.

WILLIAMS, I. *Lectures on Early Welsh Poetry*. Dublin, 1944.

HISTORICAL BACKGROUND

BIRCH, W. DE G. *Cartularium Saxonicum : a collection of charters relating to Anglo-Saxon history*. 4 vols. London, 1885-99.

BLAIR, P. H. *An Introduction to Anglo-Saxon England*. Cambridge, 1956.

COLLINGWOOD, R. G. *Roman Britain*. Revised edition. Oxford, 1949.

DUNLEAVY, G. W. ' A " De Excidio " Tradition in the Old English *Ruin* ', *PQ*, xxxviii (1959), 112-18.

EARLE, J. ' An Ancient Saxon Poem of a City in Ruins, supposed to be Bath ', *Proceedings of the Bath Natural History and Antiquities Field Club*, ii (1870-3), 259-70.

HAVERFIELD, F. ' Romano-British Somerset ', *The Victoria County History of Somerset*, i. 219-88. London, 1906.

HODGKIN, R. H. *A History of the Anglo-Saxons*. 2 vols. Third edition. Oxford, 1952.

HOTCHNER, C. A. *Wessex and Old English Poetry, with special consideration of ' The Ruin '*. New York, 1939.

KEMBLE, J. M. *Codex Diplomaticus Aevi Saxonici*. 6 vols. London, 1839-48.

LIEBERMANN, F. *Die Gesetze der Angelsachsen*. 3 vols. Halle, 1903-16.

LOT, F. *Nennius et l'Historia Brittonum*. Paris, 1934.

MOORE, C. ' The Mammalia and Other Remains from Drift Deposits in the Bath Basin ', *Proceedings of the Bath Natural History and Antiquities Field Club*, ii, No. 1 (1870-3), 42.

STENTON, SIR FRANK. *Anglo-Saxon England*. Second edition. Oxford, 1947.

WARD, J. *Romano-British Buildings and Earthworks*. London, 1911.

WHEELER, R. E. M. and ST. JOHN O'NEIL, B. H. *The Roman Baths of Bath*. Revised edition based upon original guide compiled by Alfred J. Taylor. Bath, 1954.

SUPPLEMENTARY BIBLIOGRAPHY

ANDERSON, EARL R. 'Voices in *The Husband's Message*', *Neuphilologische Mitteilungen*, lxxiv (1973), 238-46.

——'*The Husband's Message:* persuasion and the problem of "genyre"', *English Studies*, lvi (1975), 289-94.

ANDERSON, JAMES E. 'Die Deutungsmöglichkeiten des altenglischen Gedichtes *The Husband's Message*', *Neuphilologische Mitteilungen*, lxxv (1974), 402-7.

BAKER, STEWART A. '"Weal" in the Old English *Ruin*', *Notes and Queries*, x (1963), 328-9.

BAMBAS, RUDOLPH C. 'Another view of the Old English *Wife's Lament*', *JEGP*, lxii (1963), 303-9.

BATELY, JANET M. 'Time and the passing of time in *The Wanderer* and related Old English texts', *Essays and Studies,* NS xxxvii (1984), 1-15.

BESSAI, FRANK. 'Comitatus and exile in Old English poetry', *Culture*, vi (1964), 130-44.

BÖKER, UWE. 'The non-narrative structure of *The Wife's Lament:* a reconsideration of its lyric elements', in Jankowsky, K.R. and Dick, E.S. (eds), *Festschrift Für Karl Schneider.* Amsterdam, 1982, 417-29.

BOLTON, W. F. '*The Wife's Lament* and *The Husband's Message:* A reconsideration revisited', *Archiv*, ccv (1969), 337-51.

BOUMAN, A. C. 'The Old English poems *The Wife's Lament* and *The Husband's Message*', *Patterns in Old English and Old Icelandic Literature.* Leyden, 1962, 41-91.

CALDER, DANIEL G. 'Perspective and movement in *The Ruin*', *Neuphilologische Mitteilungen*, lxxii (1971), 442-5.

CAMPBELL, J. J. and ROSIER, JAMES L. (eds). *Poems in Old English.* New York, 1962.

CHASE, DENNIS. '*The Wife's Lament:* an eighth-century existential cry', *University of South Florida Language Quarterly*, xxiv (1986), 18-20.

CROSSLEY-HOLLAND, KEVIN. 'Two Old English Elegies', *Listener*, lxx (1963), 741-2. [Translations.]

CROSSLEY-HOLLAND, KEVIN (translator) and MITCHELL, BRUCE (ed.). *The Battle of Maldon and other Old English Poems.* London, 1965.

CURRY, JANE L. 'Approaches to a translation of the Anglo-Saxon *The Wife's Lament*', *Medium Aevum*, xxxv (1966), 187-98.

DAVIS, THOMAS M. 'Another view of *The Wife's Lament*', *Papers on English Language and Literature* (1965), 291-305.

DOUBLEDAY, JAMES F. '*Ruin* 8b-9a', *Notes and Queries*, xviii (1971), 124.

——'*The Ruin:* structure and theme', *JEGP*, lxxi (1972), 369-81.

DUNLEAVY, GARETH W. *Colum's Other Island.* Madison, 1960.

FITZGERALD, R. P. '*The Wife's Lament* and "The Search for the Lost Husband"', *JEGP*, lxii (1963), 769-77.

GÖLLER, KARL H. 'Die Angelsächsischen Elegien', *Germanisch-Romanische Monatsschrift*, xlv (1964), 225-41.

GREEN, MARTIN (ed.). *The Old English Elegies: New Essays in Criticism and Research.* London, Toronto, 1983.

HARRIS, JOSEPH. 'A note on "eorðscræf/eorðsele" and current interpretations of *The Wife's Lament*', *English Studies*, lviii (1977), 204-8.

HOWLETT, D. R. '*The Wife's Lament* and *The Husband's Message*', *Neuphilologische Mitteilungen*, lxxix (1977), 7-10.

HUME, KATHRYN. 'The "ruin motif" in Old English poetry', *Anglia*, lxxxxiv (1976), 339-60.

JOHNSON, LEE ANN. 'The narrative structure of *The Wife's Lament*', *English Studies*, lii (1971), 497-501.

JOHNSON, WILLIAM C., JR. '*The Ruin* as body-city riddle,' *Philological Quarterly*, lix (1980), 397-411.

KASKE, R. E. 'The reading *genyre* in *The Husband's Message* line 49'. *Medium Aevum*, xxxiii (1964), 204-6.

———'A Poem of the Cross in the Exeter Book: *Riddle 60* and *The Husband's Message*', *Traditio*, xxiii (1967), 41-71.

KEENAN, HUGH T. '*The Ruin* as Babylon', *Tennessee Studies in Literature*, xi (1966), 109-18.

KLINCK, ANNE L. 'A damaged passage in the Old English *Ruin*', *Studia Neophilologica*, lviii (1986), 165-68.

LANDRUM, MAHALA HOPE. 'A fourfold interpretation of *The Wife's Lament*'. Rutgers Dissertation. [*Dissertation Abstracts* (1964), 1915.]

LEE, ALVIN A. 'From Grendel to the Phoenix: A Critical Study of Old English Elegiac Poetry'. Toronto Dissertation, 1961.

LEE, ANNE THOMPSON. '*The Ruin*: Bath or Babylon?', *Neuphilologische Mitteilungen*, lxxiv (1973), 443-55.

LENCH, ELINOR. '*The Wife's Lament*: a poem of the living dead', *Comitatus* (1970), 3-23.

LUCAS, ANGELA M. 'The narrator of *The Wife's Lament* reconsidered', *Neuphilologische Mitteilungen*, lxx (1969), 282-97.

MALONE, KEMP. 'Two English *Frauenlieder*', *Comparative Literature*, xiv (1962), 106-17.

MITCHELL, BRUCE. 'Some problems of mood and tense in Old English', *Neophilologus*, xlix (1965), 44-6.

———'The narrator of *The Wife's Lament*', *Neuphilologische Mitteilungen*, lxxiii (1972), 222-34.

ORTON, PETER. 'The speaker in *The Husband's Message*', *Leeds Studies in English*, xii (1981), 43-56.

PILCH, H. 'The elegiac genre in Old English and early Welsh poetry', *Zeitschrift für celtische Philologie*, xxix (1964), 209-24.

REGAN, CHARLES LIONEL. '*The Wife's Lament*, 27-31 and *Kalevala*, 29: 515-532', *American Notes and Queries* (1978), 5-6.

RENOIR, ALAIN. 'Christian inversion in *The Wife's Lament*', *Studia Neophilologica*, xxxix (1977), 19-24.

———'A reading of *The Wife's Lament*', *English Studies*, lviii (1977), 4-19.

———'The least elegiac of the elegies: a contextual glance at *The Husband's Message*', *Studia Neophilologica*, liii (1981), 69-76.

RISSANEN, MATTI. 'The theme of "exile" in *The Wife's Lament*', *Neuphilologische Mitteilungen*, lxx (1969), 90-104.

SCHAEFER, URSULA. 'Two women in need of a friend: a comparison of *The Wife's Lament* and Eangyth's letter to Boniface', in Brogyanyi, B. and Krömmelbein, T. (eds), *Germanic Dialects: Linguistic and Philological Investigations*. Amsterdam, 1986, 491-524.

SCHNEIDER, KARL. '*The Husband's Message*: eine Analyse', in Mainusch, Herbert and Dietrich Rolle (eds). *Studien zur englischen Philologie: Edgar Mertner zum 70. Geburtstag*. Frankfurt, Bern, (1979), 27-59.

SHORT, DOUGLAS D. 'The Old English *Wife's Lament*: an interpretation', *Neuphilologische Mitteilungen*, lxxi (1970), 585-603.

STANLEY, E. G. '"Weal" in the Old English *Ruin*. A parallel?', *Notes and Queries*, x (1963), 405.

STEVENS, MARTIN. 'The narrator of *The Wife's Lament*', *Neuphilologische Mitteilungen*, lxix (1968), 72-90.

STRAUS, BARRIE RUTH. 'Women's words as weapons: speech as action in *The Wife's Lament*', *Texas Studies in Literature and Language*, xxiii (1981), 268-85.

SWANTON, M. J. '*The Wife's Lament* and *The Husband's Message:* A reconsideration', *Anglia*, lxxxii (1964), 269-90.

TALENTINO, ARNOLD V. 'Moral irony in *The Ruin*', *Papers in Language and Literature*, xiv (1978), 3-10.

WENTERSDORF, KARL P. 'The situation of the narrator's lord in *The Wife's Lament*', *Neuphilologische Mitteilungen*, lxxi (1970), 604-10.

——'Observations on *The Ruin*', *Medium Aevum*, xxxxvi (1977), 171-80.

——'The situation of the narrator in the Old English *Wife's Lament*', *Speculum*, lvi (1981), 492-516.

NOTE ON THE EDITED TEXT

THE text of the present edition was transcribed from the facsimile of the *Exeter Book* and afterwards collated with the manuscript and with the transcript in the British Museum (Additional MS. 9067). All the MS. abbreviations are expanded without notice. With the exception of 7 for *ond*, they are not used with any consistency. As elsewhere in the MS., accents appear sporadically and infrequently ; they occur over *no, ma, nu* WL 4, *hea* WL 30, *gad* HM 45, *stan* R 36, where the vowels are all etymologically long. Square brackets are used to indicate letters supplied by the editor either in place of the MS. reading or in addition to it ; they are also used for restorations in damaged passages. Round brackets indicate readings based upon fragmentary letters when there is doubt about their identity. Where fragments can be identified with certainty the letters are silently completed ; some faint letter fragments, not visible in the facsimile, are revealed when the MS. pages are held to the light. The number of dots in the mutilated parts of *The Husband's Message* and *The Ruin* represents the approximate number of letters missing, as estimated from the average number of letters in all the complete lines on the same page.

THE WIFE'S LAMENT

Ic þis giedd wrece   bī mē ful geōmorre,
mīnre sylfre sīð.   Ic þæt secgan mæg
hwæt ic yrmþa gebād   siþþan ic ūp [ā]wēox,
nīwes oþþe ealdes,   nō mā þonne nū ;
5 ā ic wīte wonn   mīnra wræcsīþa.
    Ǣrest mīn hlāford gewāt,   heonan of lēodum
ofer ȳþa gelāc ;   hæfde ic ūhtceare
hwǣr mīn lēodfruma   londes wǣre.
Ðā ic mē fēran gewāt   folgað sēcan,
10 winelēas wræcca   for mīnre wēaþearfe,
ongunnon þæt þæs monnes   māgas hycgan
þurh dyrne geþōht,   þæt hȳ tōdǣlden unc,
þæt wit gewīdost   in woruldrīce
lifdon lāðlīcost :   ond mec longade.
15   Hēt mec hlāford mīn   hēr eard niman ;
āhte ic lēofra lȳt   on þissum londstede,
holdra frēonda ;   forþon is mīn hyge geōmor.
    Ðā ic mē ful gemæcne   monnan funde,
heardsǣligne,   hygegeōmorne,
20 mōd mīþendne,   morþor hycgend[n]e,
blīþe gebǣro.   Ful oft wit bēotedan
þæt unc ne gedǣlde   nemne dēað āna,
ōwiht elles.   Eft is þæt onhworfen ;
is nū [fornumen]   swā hit nō wǣre,
25 frēondscipe uncer ;   s[c]eal ic feor ge nēah
mīnes felalēofan   fǣhðu drēogan.
    Heht mec mon wunian   on wuda bearwe,
under āctrēo   in þām eorðscræfe ;
eald is þes eorðsele,   eal ic eom oflongad.

3 āwēox :   *MS.* weox.
15 eard :   *MS.* heard.
20 hycgendne :   *MS.* hycgende.
24 fornumen *supplied. No gap in MS.*
25 sceal : *MS.* seal.

f. 115b 30　Sindon dena dimme,　dūna ūphēa,
　　　　　bitre burgtūnas　brērum beweaxne,
　　　　　wīc wynna lēas ;　ful oft mec hēr wrāþe begeat
　　　　　fromsīþ frēan.　Frȳnd sind on eorþan,
　　　　　lēofe lifgende　leger weardiað,
　　35　þonne ic on ūhtan　āna gonge
　　　　　under āctrēo　geond þās eorþscrafu,
　　　　　þǣr ic sitta[n] mōt　sumorlangne dæg,
　　　　　þǣr ic wēpan mæg　mīne wræcsīþas,
　　　　　earfoþa fela,　forþon ic ǣfre ne mæg
　　40　þǣre mōdceare　mīnre gerestan,
　　　　　ne ealles þæs longaþes　þe mec on þissum līfe
　　　　　　　begeat.
　　　　　Ā scyle geong mon　wesan geōmormōd,
　　　　　heard heortan geþōht ;　swylce habban sceal
　　　　　blīþe gebǣro,　ēac þon brēostceare,
　　45　sinsorgna gedreag.　Sȳ æt him sylfum gelong
　　　　　eal his worulde wyn,　sȳ ful wīde fāh
　　　　　feorres folclondes　þæt mīn frēond siteð
　　　　　under stānhliþe,　storme behrīmed,
　　　　　wine wērigmōd　wætre beflōwen
　　50　on drēorsele,　drēogeð sē mīn wine
　　　　　micle mōdceare ;　hē gemon tō oft
　　　　　wynlicran wīc.　Wā bið þām þe sceal
　　　　　of langoþe　lēofes ābīdan.

　　　　37 sittan : *MS.* sittam.

THE HUSBAND'S MESSAGE

f. 123a

Nū ic onsundran þē   secgan wille
. . . . (n) trēocyn.   Ic tūdre āwēox ;
in mec æld[a] . . . . sceal
ellor londes setta(n) . . . . lc,
5 sealte strēamas . . . . sse.
Ful oft ic on bātes [bōsme] . . . . gesōhte,
þǣr mec mondryhten   mīn . . . .
ofer hēah h[a]fu ;   eom nū hēr cumen
on cēolþele,   ond nū cunnan scealt
10 hū þū ymb mōdluf[a]n   mīnes frēan
on hyge hycge.   Ic gehātan dear
þæt þū þǣr tīrfæste   trēowe findest.
    Hwæt, þec þonne biddan hēt,   sē þisne bēam
        āgrōf,
þæt þū sinchroden   sylf gemunde
15 on gewitlocan   wordbēotunga
þe git on ǣrdagum   oft gesprǣcon,
þenden git mōston   on meoduburgum
eard weardigan,   ān lond būgan,
frēondscype fremman.   Hine fǣhþo ādrāf
20 of sigeþēode.   Heht nū sylfa þē
lustum lǣra[n]   þæt þū lagu drēfde,

f. 123b

siþþan þū gehȳrde   on hliþes ōran
galan geōmorne   gēac on bearwe.
Ne lǣt þū þec siþþan   sīþes getwǣfan,
25 lāde gelettan,   līfgendne monn.
    Ongin mere sēcan,   mǣwes eþel ;
onsite sǣnacan,   þæt þū sūð heonan
ofer merelāde   monnan findest,
þǣr sē þēoden is   þīn on wēnum.
30 Ne mæg him [on] worulde   willa [gelimpan]
māra on gemyndum,   þæsþe hē mē sægde,

8 hafu : *MS.* hofu.   10 mōdlufan : *MS.* modlufun.
21 lǣran : *MS.* lǣram.
30 gelimpan *supplied. No gap in MS.*
49

þonne inc geunne   alwaldend God,
[þæt git] ætsomne   siþþan mōtan
secgum ond gesīþum   s[inc brytnian],
35 næglede bēagas.   Hē genōh hafað
fǣdan gold[es], ...
[geon]d elþēode   ēþel healde,
fægre folda[n] . . . .
[hold]ra hæleþa,   þēahþe hēr mīn win(e)
40 . . . .
nȳde gebǣded, nacan ūt āþrong,
ond on ȳþa gel(a)g[u   āna] sceolde
faran on flotweg,   forðsīþes georn
mengan merestrēamas.   Nū sē mon hafað
45 wēan oferwunnen ;   nis him wilna gād,
ne mēara, ne māðma,   ne meododrēama
ǣnges ofer eorþan   eorlgestrēona,
þēodnes dohtor,   gif hē þīn beneah.
Ofer eald gebēot   incer twēga,
50 gehȳre ic ætsomne   . S . R . geador
. EA . W . ond . M .   āþe benemnan
þæt hē þā wǣre   ond þā winetrēowe,
be him lifgendum   lǣstan wolde,
þe git on ǣrdagum   oft gesprǣconn.

THE RUIN

f. 123b   Wrǣtlic is þes wealstān,   wyrde gebrǣcon ;
f. 124a   burgstede burston ;   brosnað enta geweorc.
      Hrōfas sind gehrorene, hrēorge torras,
      hr[un]geat berofen, hrīm on līme,
   5 scearde scūrbeorge   scorene gedrorene
      ældo undereotone.   Eorðgrāp hafað
      waldendwyrhtan,   forweorone geleorene,
      heard gripe hrūsan,   oþ hund cnēa
      werþēoda gewitan.   Oft þæs wāg gebād,
  10 rǣghār ond rēadfāh,   rīce æfter ōþrum,
      ofstonden under stormum ;   stēap gēap gedrēas.
      Wōrað gīet sē[o] . . . . (r)um gehēa[w]en ;
      fēlon u . . . . e
      grimme gegrunden . . . .
  15 . . . . (rð) scān   heo. . . . .
      . . . . g orþonc,   ǣrsceaft . . . .
      . . . . g   lāmrindum bēag.
      Mōd mo[nade]   myne swiftne gebrægd ;
      hwætrēd in hringas,   hygerōf gebond
  20 weallwalan wīrum   wundrum tōgædre.
      Beorht wǣron burgrǣced,   burnsele monige,
      hēah horngestrēon,   hereswēg micel,
      meodoheall monig   mondrēama full,
      oþþæt þæt onwende   wyrd sēo swīþe.
  25 Crungon walo wīde,   cwōman wōldagas ;
      swylt eall fornōm   secgrōf[ra] wera ;
      wurdon hyra wīgsteal   wēstenstaþolas.
      Brosnade burgsteall ;   bētend crungon,
      hergas tō hrūsan.   Forþon þās hofu drēorgiað
  30 ond þæs tēaforgēapa   tigelum sceādeð

---

4 hrungeat : *MS.* hrim geat.   torras *is repeated in the MS.*
after hrim geat.
12 gehēawen : *MS.* geheapen.
26 secgrōfra : *MS.* secg rof.

f. 124b   hrōstbēages [h]rōf. Hryre wong gecrong,
          gebrocen tō beorgum, þǣr iū beorn monig,
          glædmōd ond goldbeorht, gleoma gefrætwe[d],
          wlonc ond wīngāl, wīghyrstum scān ;
35 seah on sinc, on sylfor, on searogimmas,
          on ēad, on ǣht, on eorcanstān,
          on þās beorhtan burg brādan rīces.
            Stānhofu stōdan ; strēam hāte wearp
          wīdan wylme ; weal eall befēng
40 beorhtan bōsme ; þǣr þā baþu wǣron,
          hāt on hreþre ; þæt wæs hȳðelic.
          Lēton þonne gēotan (þ) . . . .
          ofer hārne stān, hāte strēamas
          un(d) . . . .
45 oþ þæt hringmere. Hāte (st) . . . .
          . . . . þǣr þā baþu wǣron.
          þonne is . . . .
          . . . . re ; þæt is cynelic þing,
          hū sē b . . . . burg. (str) . . .

31 hrōf : *MS.* rof.
33 gefrætwed : *MS.* gefrætweð.

NOTES

THE WIFE'S LAMENT

3. The second half-line is metrically defective in the MS. A lightly stressed syllable is required between *ūp* and *wēox*. Sievers's reading *ūp [ā]wēox* (*Beiträge*, x. 516) is followed by all who emend. *Riddles* 9.10, 10.3, and 73.1 have *āwēox* in a similar metrical position ; cf. also *Elene* 1225 : *ūp āwēoxe*.

4. **niwes** and **ealdes** are genitive forms of the adjectives *nīwe* and *eald*, used adverbially. A number of adverbs of time are formed from adjectives in this way, e.g. *dæglanges*, *simbles* ; cf. Campbell, § 668.

5. **wīte wonn.** Roeder (p. 113) and Schücking (*ZfdA*, xlviii. 438, but not in his *Kleines as. Dichterbuch*) take MS. *wīte* as a verb. Emendation is unnecessary if *wīte* is taken as a noun ' torment ' and *wonn* as the pret. sg. of the verb *winnan*, ' to undergo, suffer ', as in *Genesis* 1014 : *wīte winnan* and *Guthlac* 469 : *wīte āwunne*.

7. **ūhtceare.** The period just before dawn rather than dawn itself is meant by *ūhte*, as in Alfred's translation of Gregory's *Pastoral Care* (ed. H. Sweet, E.E.T.S., Original Series, No. 50, 1872, p. 461, line 2), where *ūhtan* translates *profundioribus horis noctis*, while dawn itself is indicated by *dægrēd* ; cf. *on ūhtan ǣr dægrēde* (*Christ and Satan* 463-4). Early morning appears to have been a time of special misery ; cf. E. G. Stanley, ' Old English Poetic Diction and the Interpretation of *The Wanderer*, *The Seafarer* and *The Penitent's Prayer* ', *Anglia*, lxxiii (1955), 434-5.

9. **folgað** appears to have been a legal term in Old English, denoting the service due by a retainer to his lord ; cf. F. Liebermann, *Die Gesetze der Angelsachsen* (Halle, 1906), ii. 73, s.v. *folgoðe* and 424, s.v. *Gefolge*, 2b. Elsewhere in Old English poetry the noun has this meaning in *Deor* 38 and *Solomon and Saturn* 371. *Folgað sēcan*, therefore, indicates that the woman went in search of her husband, referred to as her lord in lines 6, 8 and 15.

14. **lāðlicost** is taken by Schücking (*ZfdA*, xlviii. 442) to mean ' most hatefully (to each other) '. The adverb *lāðlīce* and the adjective *lāðlic*, however, normally refer to things or conditions, rather than people ; for personal relationships *lāðe* and *lāð* are used. Hence *lāðlīcost* means ' in most wretched fashion ', a reference to the manner in which the two were to live that is borne out by the woman's own situation and by her fears for her husband's plight in the closing lines.

15. **hēr eard niman.** The MS. has *her heard niman*. Grein (*Germania*, x. 422) takes the first two words together as a compound noun, an unusual dialectal spelling of *heargeard*, ' dwelling in a grove ', and supports his interpretation in his edition (*Bibliothek der Angelsächsischen*

Poesie, ii. 414) by reference to the woman's situation *on wuda bearwe* (27). In support of the form **hearg* he cites OHG *haruc*, ' grove ' ; but OE *hearh*, like ON *hörgr*, means ' idol ' or ' temple '. Miss Kershaw and Greenfield take *heard* as an epithet of *hláford*, meaning ' stern ' or ' cruel ' ; but the separation of the adjective from its noun by both the possessive pronoun *mín* and the adverb *hér* is unnatural ; cf. *Beowulf* 375-6. Conybeare takes *heard* adverbially and Sedgefield regards it as qualifying an understood noun meaning ' lot '. But these are strained constructions, and probably the best solution is emendation of *heard* to *eard*. Scribal error resulting from the influence of the preceding word would account for the intrusive *h*, or else the phenomenon whereby *h* is often inserted without etymological justification before words beginning with a vowel ; cf. Sievers-Brunner, § 217, Anmerkung 1. The idiomatic phrase *eard niman*, ' to take up one's abode ', occurs in *Psalm* 131, 15.3 (*Paris Psalter*) : *þǽr ic eard nime*, where it translates *hic habitabo*, in *Christ* 63 : *nimeð eard in pé*, and in *Guthlac* 3172 : *somudeard niman*. The metrical structure is similar to that in *Maxims* II, 64 : *hider under hrófas þe þæt hér for sóð*, where *hér* carries the alliteration, even in the presence of a noun in the same half-line. There is no justification, therefore, for passing over *hér* in favour of *heard* as the alliterating word, especially as *hér* is also the first stressed syllable in the half-line. Consequently emendation of *heard* to *eard* is desirable on metrical as on other grounds, in order to avoid double alliteration in the second half-line, contrary to the established practice of Old English poets.

16. **léofra lýt** is a form of understatement frequently applied to exiles and outcasts in Old English poetry. The woman means that she has no friends at all, as do other lonely persons like the *winelēas hæle* in *The Fortunes of Men* 30-2, where the context makes this meaning plain.

17. The adverb **forþon,** ' therefore ', indicates that the woman's sadness is caused by her lack of friends. Some editors begin a new sentence with *forþon*, put a comma after *geómor* and take *ðá* (18) as a conjunction meaning ' since ' or ' when '. They assume that the *forþon* clause refers to the lines which follow it, and Lawrence (*JGP*, iv. 463) and Miss Kershaw give to the adverb the meaning ' assuredly '. Such a meaning is valid when the comment introduced by *forþon* is parenthetic, as in *The Wanderer* 37, 64 and *The Seafarer* 27, but is precluded here if the *ðá* clause of reason or time is made to depend on the *forþon* clause.

18-21. This clause has usually been taken as subordinate. But it cannot depend on *is* in the preceding line (see Note to line 17), nor on *béotedan* (21), because there is no inversion of *wit* and *béotedan* as there would be following a subordinate clause, and because the customary place for a *ful oft . . .* construction is at the beginning of a sentence. The verb *funde* is introduced very late for a principal clause, perhaps in order to be as close as possible to the adjectives and present participles which follow it and which are to be taken predicatively. Lawrence

(*MP*, v. 388-92) believes that these epithets refer to the characteristics of the husband which made him *ful gemæcne*, ' a very congenial mate ', for the woman ; but it is difficult to believe that present participles with direct objects postulating action can refer to permanent characteristics. Miss Kershaw takes the adjectives in line 19 as qualifying *gemæcne* and the participles as predicative, but the distinction is an arbitrary one, for which there is no warrant in the word order.

21. **blīþe gebǣro** is taken by some editors as the opening of a new sentence, but since *ful oft* usually begins a sentence, it is preferable to take *blīþe gebǣro* as an instrumental phrase dependent on both the preceding participles, meaning ' with cheerful outward mien '. Unwillingness to accept -*o* as a dative ending in *gebǣro* led Ettmüller and Sedgefield to suggest emendation to *gebǣrum* ; but the final *o* can be explained as a neuter dative singular ending agreeing with the adjective *blīþe* which must be masculine or neuter instrumental. There is a cognate noun in OHG *gibāri*, which is of the same declension as OHG *menigī*, cognate with OE *menigu* ; it is likely therefore that *gebǣre* should be declined like *menigu*, which, with other Gmc. feminine -*īn* stems, was remodelled in OE after the *ō* stems, with later generalising of the nominative singular ending in *u* or *o* throughout the singular (cf. Sievers-Brunner, § 280). *Gebǣro* cannot, however, be feminine. Toller suggests that a neuter noun may be surmised from extant plural forms, and notes that OS *gibāri* is neuter. It is probable that the noun changed its gender by analogy partly with neuter *i* stems with nominative and accusative plurals in *u* or *o*, and partly with the many feminine *i* stem nouns with the prefix *ge*- which became neuter either entirely or in part. The same phrase occurs in the accusative in line 44.

24. A word is required to complete the metrical pattern of the first half-line. The past participle *geworden* suggested by Schücking (*ZfdA*, xlviii. 443) satisfies the metre and grammar of the context, but *fornumen*, or a similar participle of a verb of deprivation, would be equally suitable.

26. **fǣhðu** is a technical term used to describe a state of feud ; cf. Liebermann, *op. cit.* ii, 67, s.v. *fǣhðe*, and 320, s.v. *Blutrache*. It cannot, therefore, refer to hostility of the husband towards his wife ; personal enmity is generally expressed in Old English by *hete* or its compounds. *Felalēofan* must be taken as an objective genitive, indicating that the woman must suffer the consequences of her husband's feud with a third party.

28-36. The woman's dwelling under the oak tree is referred to by **eorðscræfe** (28), **eorðsele** (29), and the plural **eorþscrafu** (36). That a cave or succession of caves is meant is suggested by the occurrence as dwelling-places of *eorðscræfu*, with the variant *moldern*—a compound similar in formation to *eorðsele*—in *Andreas* 803. It is unusual, however, for a natural feature to be described as *eald* (29) in Old English. This epithet is generally used of man-made objects, and is applied to *eorðsele* in its only other occurrence, with reference to the dragon's lair in *Beowulf* 2410 and 2515, which is identified as a chambered barrow by G. E. Daniel, *The Prehistoric Chamber Tombs of England and Wales* (Cambridge 1950), p. 22, n. 6. There are precedents for the use of barrows as solitary dwellings in Anglo-Saxon times, namely the site of St. Guthlac's cell in Crowland, and the *hoga* of Cutteslowe, north of Oxford ; see *Felix's Life of St. Guthlac*, edited by B. Colgrave (Cambridge 1956), pp. 182-4. It is possible, therefore, that the woman's habitation is a chambered barrow. Her use of the definitive *þām* (28) suggests that the *eorðscræfe* is an outstanding feature of the landscape.

30. **dena . . . dūna.** The occurrence together of these words in *Riddle* 27.3 also, suggests a common antithetical phrase such as modern English ' hills and dales '.

31. **burgtūnas** is a compound not found elsewhere in Old English literature, although it must have been commonly used for place-names to judge by the numbers of Burtons, Broughtons and Bourtons derived from it. It is likely that each element bore its earlier sense, *burg* meaning ' fortification ' and *tūn* ' fence or enclosure ', the whole meaning an enclosure round a fortification, possibly an ancient earthwork (see A. H. Smith, *English Place-Name Elements*, Part I (Cambridge 1956), s.v. *burh-tūn*). The epithet *biter* has probably the meaning ' sharp ' as in *Beowulf*, of arrows (1746) and of a sword (2704), and refers to the briars which have grown over the protecting walls of the cave or mound, although the abstract meaning ' bitter ' may be intended as well.

32. **wrāþe begeat.** According to Miss Rickert (*MP*, ii. 367, n. 2), *wrāþe* may be an adjective, adverb, or even a noun ; but from its position it is most probably an adverb, meaning ' grievously '. The woman states that the departure of her lord grievously laid hold of her. The concrete subject used for vividness contains the abstract idea and implies the thought of her lord's departure. The construction is similar to that in *The Seafarer* 6-7 ; *þǣr mec oft bigeat/nearo nihtwaco*.

34. **leger weardiað.** Most editors have translated *on eorþan* as ' in the ground ' and *leger* as ' grave ', taking *lēofe lifgende* to mean ' dear ones while still living '. It is, however, much less clumsy to take *on eorþan* as ' on earth ' and *leger* as ' bed ' as in Miss Kershaw's translation. The reference to *frýnd* (33) lying abed, in contrast to her own loneliness, suggests the meaning ' lovers ' for *frýnd* here, for she is thinking of the relationship between herself and her husband.

35. **þonne** is probably the conjunction ' while ' rather than the adverb ' then ', because of the close linking of the ideas which follow it with the preceding lines, and because of the delayed introduction of the finite verb. Similarly *þǣr* (37, 38) is to be translated ' where ' and *forþon* (39) ' because '.

37. **sumorlangne dæg.** It is uncertain whether the speaker means that it was literally summer, or whether she is using the word figuratively. She may be implying, like the speaker in *Juliana* 495-7, that

she has troubles enough to occupy her throughout the longest day, a summer's day. Cf. the opposite use of *winterstund* to mean ' a short time ' in *Genesis* B 370.

42-5. These lines contain a gnomic passage outlining conduct which a man should display, as indicated by the use of the only finite verbs, **scyle** (42) and **sceal** (43) ; cf. *Ā scyle pā rincas gerǣdan lǣdan/ond him ǣtsomne swēfan* (*Maxims* I, 177-8). The moods of the verb are usually differentiated with respect to human behaviour, *sceal* being preferred to list fundamental qualities, and *scyle* to indicate desirable qualities ; cf. *The Seafarer* 109-11 : *Stīeran mon sceal strongum mōde . . . scyle monna gehwylc mid gemete healdan*, also the alternation between *skyli* and *skal* in the first lines of stanzas 93 and 94 of the *Hávamál* and the use of *scyle* in *The Order of the World* 17, 98. Another gnomic feature is the use of the impersonal *mon*, commonly found with *scyle* and *sceal*. Somewhat similar sentiments are expressed in *Hávamál*, stanza 15.

42. **geōmormōd.** Since the gnomic form of the passage indicates an attitude of mind here rather than a passing mood, a meaning such as Toller's ' sad of soul ' or Lawrence's (*JGP*, iv. 389) ' serious of mind ' would be appropriate ; cf. the old warrior, experienced in the struggles of men, a man with a *grim sefa*, who is described as *geōmormōd* in *Beowulf* 2044.

43. As Miss Kershaw suggests, there are two ways in which **heard heortan gepōht** may possibly be construed, either with *scyle wesan* (42) or with *habban sceal* (43). The latter is unlikely because *swylce* ' likewise ' separates the phrase from *habban sceal*, making *ā scyle . . . gepōht* one clause to which *habban sceal . . . gedreag* is likened. Hence *heard*, like *geōmormōd*, is to be predicated with *scyle . . . wesan*.

The meaning of *heard* when applied to thoughts is ' steadfast, constant ' ; cf. *Guthlac* 977-8 : *mōd swīpe heard/elnes ānhydig*.

44. **ēac pon** is a compound adverb meaning ' moreover ', ' besides ' ; it glosses Latin *ceterum* (*Narratiunculae Anglice Conscriptae*, edited by Cockayne (London, 1861), p. 9, line 14).

45. **sinsorgna gedreag**, ' a multitude of constant sorrows ', has a parallel in *Precepts* 76 : *tornsorgna ful*.

45b-47. **sȳ . . . sȳ . . .** Lawrence (*JGP*, iv. 402-3, n. 2) takes these lines with the preceding, as part of the gnomic construction. His solution raises difficulties over the relationship of the *pæt* clause in lines 47 ff., which, like many other editors, he avoids by emending *pæt* to *pǣr*. Stefanovíc (*loc. cit.* 420-2) attaches line 45b to the preceding lines, making *gedreag* the subject of *sȳ* ; but such a clause has no connection with the *scyle, sceal* formulas and the subject *gedreag* does not suit the idiomatic *æt him gelong*, discussed below. These objections do not apply if the lines are taken with the following *pæt* clause, where the speaker reverts from the general to the particular. The verb *sȳ* in lines 45 and 46 may be taken as third person singular imperative, as by most early editors, or as optatives containing an alternative hypothesis as Modern High German *sei . . . sei . . .*, 'whether . . . or . . .'; cf. *sȳ pēr māre landes, sȳ pēr lǣsse* in F. E. Harmer, *Anglo-Saxon Writs* (Manchester 1952), Writ No. 107, p. 395, line 9, and also Writ No. 26, p. 182, line 11. This construction has the advantage of making clear the hypothetical nature of the speaker's reconstruction of her husband's circumstances, for she has no knowledge of his whereabouts (cf. lines 7-8). Miss Kershaw states that the second hypothesis is complicated by the introduction of a fresh consideration, and that the addition of the *þæt* clause causes the suppression of the verb of the original clause, or rather, converts it from a personal to an impersonal use. But the circumstances of the *þæt* clause illustrate the plight of one who is *fāh*, 'outcast', and *þæt . . . drēorsele* is therefore a complete clause, an integral part of the second hypothesis, dependent on *sȳ* (46). *Sȳ . . . wyn* is one concessive clause, *sȳ . . . drēorsele* another, with *drēogeð* and *gemon* the verbs in the principal clauses. The lack of a specified subject in the second hypothesis, after the personal note in the first, makes it certain that the construction is to be taken impersonally, rather than that the personal pronoun *hē* should be supplied, in which case *sȳ hē ful wīde fāh* would have been expected.

45. **æt . . . gelong.** In this idiom *gelong*, 'belonging to', has the specialised application 'dependent on'; cf. *Beowulf* 1376-7 : *Nū is sē rǣd gelang/eft æt þē ānum*, and *Guthlac* 312-3.

46. **worulde wyn.** Schücking's emendation (*ZfdA*, xlviii. 446) to a compound *woruld-wyn* is unnecessary ; cf. *worolde wynne* in *Beowulf* 1080.

49-50. Miss Kershaw comments on the vagueness of the scene and suggests that it may refer to a flooded ruin or to a cave on the coast to which access can be obtained only by water. But it is perhaps simpler to take the force of *be-* in *beflōwen* as indicating an island.

52. The poem closes with a gnomic reflection. Sedgefield points out that the masculine demonstrative is occasionally used with reference to a feminine noun, and compares *Beowulf* 1260, 1344. But the point of this exclamation is its impersonal application, and the reference can be applied to either sex. That we have a gnomic formula is shown by the occurrence of the identical words in *Beowulf* 183-4 : *wā bið þǣm ðe sceal/þurh slīðne nīð sāwle bescūfan.*

53. **of langoþe.** Emendation of *of* to *on* as suggested by Grein (*Germania*, x. 422) is unnecessary, if *of* be taken to denote a cause or reason, the phrase meaning 'out of longing'. Verbs of rest in Old English often had a rather more active sense than they now possess.

2. The gap in the text before **trēocyn** is caused by the lacuna in folio 123. *Trēocyn* is probably to be taken as part of a prepositional phrase dependent on *secgan wille*. There is room for both a preposition and a short adjective. If the preposition took the dative, the letter fragment would belong to *m*, part of the adjectival neuter dative ending -*um*, and the noun would require expansion, as in Mackie's *ymb þisum trēocyn[ne]*, the only restoration of those proposed which conforms to the space available in the MS. An accusative construction is not, however, to be ruled out, since there may have been no letters missing in the hole in the margin.

The second half-line appears to be a self-contained sentence, for the phrase **in mec** in line 3 looks forward to *sceal . . . settan* rather than back to *āwēox* with which it would be tautological. As it stands, the statement, ' I grew up from childhood ', may appear unnecessary, but the whole introductory passage has a highly formal tone.

3-4. In the MS. only the rather blurred top of *in* remains, but the British Museum transcript of the *Exeter Book* enables the letters to be identified. The first two letters of the word after *mec* are badly smudged, but a low *e*, as the second part of an *æ* digraph, is clearly discernible when the folio is held to the light. The use of low *e* indicates that a letter with an upstroke followed. Beyond, the hook of a *d* is clear, and, two spaces further on, an upstroke.

Krapp-Dobbie ends the first half-line with *sceal* and takes *ellor londes* as the second half-line. Such an arrangement does not make sufficient allowance for the missing text, about twelve letters. These would suffice to complete both half-lines, as is illustrated by my suggested restoration : *in mec æld[a bearn ærende] sceal*. Difficulty with the phrase *in mec* is resolved if it be taken with *settan* in the idiomatic construction meaning ' to place in my charge ' ; s.v. B-T, *settan*, II. The Krapp-Dobbie arrangement of line 4 :

settan . . . . sealte strēamas

allows no more than part of the first half-line for the missing text, a space much too small, even when the minimum number of missing letters is taken into consideration.

6. A noun in the dative, dependent on *on*, has been lost after *bātes*, possibly *bōsme*, as in similar constructions in *Genesis* 1306, 1332 and *The Battle of Brunanburh* 27. Mackie and Krapp-Dobbie put *ful oft ic on bātes* in the previous line, leaving *gesōhte* at the end of this line. Three-quarters of a line of verse is, however, an excessive space to allow for the maximum of seventeen letters likely to be missing, having regard to the fact that the contents of the gap would, by virtue of such an

arrangement, have had to include at least three separate words to obtain the minimum alliterative pattern. The equivalent of half a line of verse, requiring fourteen letters, entirely fills the space available in my restoration : *Ful oft ic on bātes [bōsme byrig þær] gesōhte.*

7. Most editors, following Grein, restore *onsende* after *mīn*, but, as Mackie states in a footnote in his edition, the tail of *s* would still be visible in the MS. There could have been no letter with a downstroke from the second onwards. There is room for about seven letters, and the context appears to require a verb in the preterite singular. The construction whereby the possessive adjective comes after the noun it qualifies, in a different half-line, and is emphasised by alliteration, is similar to that in line 29.

8. **h[a]fu.** Sievers's emendation of MS. *hofu* to *hafu*, in *Beiträge*, x. 516, has been followed by many editors, though not by Mackie and Krapp-Dobbie. *Hofu*, ' buildings ', is out of place in a context of voyaging. With *ofer hēah hafu*, ' across the high seas ', compare *hēan strēamas* in *The Seafarer* 34.

9. **scealt.** Grein emends to *sceal*, but the MS. reading makes good sense if *þū* is understood as the subject. Repetition of *nū* so close to its occurrence in line 8 appears unidiomatic, and its presence in line 9 may be in mistake for *þū*.

10. **frēan.** Sievers, *Beiträge*, x. 479, emends to *frigan* for metrical reasons. But, if *frēan* is taken to be a contraction of earlier **frēgean*, with the preservation of the archaic pronunciation, the half-line can be scanned as a normal A type ; cf. *Deniga frēan* in *Beowulf* 271, 359, 1680.

12. Miss Kershaw suggests that the line *hwær ic tīrfæste trēowe funde* in *Psalm* 100.6 in the *Paris Psalter* may be a reminiscence of this line. Support for the suggestion is to be found by a comparison with the Vulgate text, where the absence of any corresponding Latin clause shows this line to be an interpolation by the Old English writer.

13. **Hwæt.** This exclamation is frequently used to introduce a change of topic or tone in a speech, as in *Beowulf* 942.

14. **sinchroden.** The use of this epithet suggests not only that the person addressed is a woman, but that she is a lady of rank ; cf. the use of the similar epithet *goldhroden* in *Beowulf* 614, 640, 1948, 2025, where the reference is always to a queen or princess.

16. This line is repeated as the last line of the poem, with the spelling variant *-nn* instead of *-n* in *gesprǣcon*.

17. **meoduburgum.** The only other occurrence of this compound is in *Judith* 167. The meaning is almost certainly ' cities containing mead-halls '. From place-names, though not from literature, there is evidence that Old English contained compounds with three elements, of the type **meoduhealburg* ; cf. Beerfostal from *bǣre, fore* and *steall*. and Saltonstall from *Salhtūnstall* (A. H. Smith, *English Place-Name Elements*). But the use of metonymy, i.e. ' mead ' for ' mead-hall ', may well have led to the formation of new compounds ; cf. the similar

formations in *Beowulf, medustig* (924), ' path near the mead-hall ' and *meodowong* (1643), ' plain beside the mead-hall '.

18. **eard weardigan,** an idiomatic phrase meaning ' to dwell ', is found in a similar context in *Christ* 772 : *þenden wē on eorðan eard weardigen.*

19. **frēondscype** is also used in *The Wife's Lament* 25, of the relationship between man and woman.

20. There is some ellipsis here. **Sylfa** stands in apposition to **hē** understood. In full the construction would be *(hē) heht (mec) nū sylfa þē lustum lǣran,* ' he himself bade me now joyfully inform you '.

21. Grein's emendation to *listum* in his edition (ii. 414) is unnecessary. The adverbial use of the dative plural of *lust* is substantiated elsewhere ; cf. *Genesis* 16 and *The Metres of Boethius* 9.44.

lagu drēfde. The conception of a voyage as a disturbing of the waters appears elsewhere in Old English poetry. The same phrase is used in *Riddle* 22.16 ; cf. *drēfan dēop wæter* in *Beowulf* 1904.

23. **geōmorne gēac.** The cuckoo figures in the folk-lore and literature of many peoples as the harbinger of summer ; it also foretells sorrow, sickness and death, as shown by Sieper (pp. 70-7). Where the bird appears elsewhere in Old English poetry, it is explicitly as the herald of summer ; cf. *Guthlac* 744 : *gēacas gēar budon* and *The Seafarer* 53-4 : *gēac monað geōmran reorde/singeð sumeres weard.* As in our poem, the cuckoo in *The Seafarer* is a signal for departure on a voyage. It appears that the conceptions of the cuckoo as herald of summer, and of summer as a season of calm seas safe for voyaging, have been conflated. In an early Irish poem on the advent of summer ' the loud hardy cuckoo calls, welcome noble summer ! . . . the smooth sea flows, season when the ocean falls asleep ' (K. Jackson, *Early Celtic Nature Poetry* (Cambridge, 1935), p. 23).

A striking feature common to both *The Husband's Message* and *The Seafarer* is the sad call of the cuckoo, which is prevalent in the literature and folk-lore of a number of Indo-European peoples, particularly the Celts and Slavs ; but outside these poems it is found among the Germanic peoples only in a Swedish popular proverb (cited by O. S. Anderson, *The Seafarer, an Interpretation*, p. 23), according to which a cuckoo heard from the north foreshadows sorrow, and from the south, death. The proverb suggests that the sad cuckoo may have been known to Germanic tradition, but the Old English elegies are unique in their use of it as a literary motif ; it is used, moreover, in a manner which has affinities with Old Welsh poetry, its significance in which has been pointed out by Professor Ifor Williams in *Lectures in Early Welsh Poetry* (Dublin 1944), pp. 12-13. For the Welsh poets the cuckoo was a symbol of separation from loved ones. It is this aspect of the bird which is particularly appropriate to *The Husband's Message.*

24. **þec** is omitted by Craigie. It is, however, required as the object of the infinitives *getwǣfan* and *gelettan* ; cf. the similar construction

with *gelettan* in *Guthlac* 358-9. The nominative *þū*, which immediately precedes, illustrates the Old English custom of inserting the pronoun after the imperative when the latter is accompanied by an adverb of negation.

27. **þæt.** The conjunction has here the meaning 'so that as a result', or 'until that'; cf. *Andreas* 786-8: *Gewāt hē þā faran ... þæt hē on Mambre becōm;* s.v. B-T, *þæt* III (1). The idea of purpose is unlikely, because *findest* is in the indicative, not the subjunctive, mood.

30. Two letters appear to have been erased before **worulde.** It is generally assumed that they constituted a preposition, probably *on*, although it is claimed by Krapp-Dobbie that a preposition is not absolutely necessary here. Trautmann (*Anglia*, xvi. 217) suggests that the scribe wrote *woru* and then scratched out all but the second stroke of the *u*, for *on* to be written in later; but there is not room for *woru* to have been written within the limits of the erasure. *On* may possibly have been erased by someone who believed that *worulde* depended in the genitive upon *willa*, a construction similar to *worulde wyn* in *The Wife's Lament* 46; such a belief would be supported by the absence of an infinitive on which *on worulde* could depend. As it stands in the MS. the line is metrically incomplete. Since *mæg* lacks an infinitive, the restoration of *gelimpan*, first suggested by Grein, has been adopted by most editors. The accidental omission of the infinitive at some stage in the transmission of the poem could have obscured the function of *on* before *worulde*, and may thus have prompted its erasure.

31. **mãra on gemyndum.** The poetic plural *gemyndum*, with singular meaning, appears several times in Old English poetry; cf. *Juliana* 36: *mãra in gemyndum*.

32. **alwaldend God** is the only overt Christian reference in the poem.

33. With this line the lacuna begins to affect the text on f. 123b. The final letter of *god* is visible only in part, but the distinctive initial hook establishes its identity. Beyond the gap are the loop of tall *e* and part of a ligature with a preceding letter, which are clearly part of *æ* in *ætsomne*. The restoration *þæt git*, put forward by Ettmüller, has been followed by all who attempt restoration. The conjunction *þæt* follows from the imperative *geunne*. In the following clause, both *ætsomne* and *mōtan* indicate the need for a plural subject, for which the dual pronoun *git* is a probable choice, since the talk is of the husband and wife, already referred to as *inc* in the previous line; *þæt git* would fit the space available if *þæt* were in its common abbreviated form.

34. The word after **gesīþum** began with a downstroke, which thickens towards the top in the manner of *f* or *s*. The latter is more likely because of the necessity for alliteration with *secgum* and *gesīþum* in the previous half-line. The only restorations completely acceptable on paleographic grounds are Grein's *sinc brytnian* and Kluge's *sinc gedǣlan*. Either would fit the context, but *brytnian* is the usual verb in similar contexts in Old English poetry; cf. *Beowulf* 2383: *sinc*

brytnade. Blackburn's restoration, *sinc ūt āgifan*, fits only with some cramping of the words.

35. The lower portions of the letters *næg* and *beag* in **nægledе bēagas** are missing, but collation of the remains in the MS. with the readings in the transcript removes any doubt about the identity of all but the *g* in *næglede*, where the transcript has *t*. The top of *g*, however, is very similar to *t* in Old English manuscripts and the well-authenticated *næglede* is to be preferred to the unknown alternative, *nætlede*.

36. Many editors emend **fǣdan** to *fǣttan*, which they relate to Gothic *fētjan* ' to burnish '. Krapp-Dobbie retains the MS. form and accounts for it as a variant spelling. *Fǣdan*, however, can be explained as the inflected form of the past participle of the verb whose 3 singular present indicative *fǣhit* glosses Latin *pingit* in the Epinal and Corpus Glossaries (see H. Sweet, *The Oldest English Texts* (London 1885), p. 86, line 785 and p. 87, line 1582) ; the contracted preterite plural *fǣdun*, ' they painted ', also appears in these glossaries (p. 88, line 797 and p. 85, line 1504) ; cf. Campbell, § 247(d).

37. The final letter *d* of a word lost in the gap is preceded by a fragment which is usually identified as part of *i*. It cannot be identified from the facsimile, but the MS. indicates conclusively that it is the shoulder of *n* or *r*. The presence of *genōh* (35) and the subjunctive form of the verb *healde* (37) indicate that the beginning of a clause of purpose has been lost. That its subject was probably *hē* is indicated both by the preceding main clause (35b-36a) and by the singular inflexion of *healde*. Since *ēþel* is the object of *healde*, *elþēode* is to be taken as part of an adverbial phrase, preceded by a preposition which ended in *-nd* or *-rd*. It is most probable that this preposition was *geond*, with the meaning ' among ', as in *Andreas* 25 and *Daniel* 573. If *þæt hē* and *geond* are restored on each side of the gap, space is left for one or two words, containing two stressed syllables, beginning with *f* to alliterate with *fǣdan* (or *g* with *goldes*) in line 36. These words, or elements of a compound noun perhaps, may have been a variant of *fǣdan goldes* as in Grein's restoration *feohgest-rēona,/þeah hē on*, or Blackburn's *fēos 7 hringa,/þā he mid*. They could, however, have consisted of a restatement of the subject, as in Sedge-field's restoration *Frēa sylfa cwæð/þæt hē on*, although by beginning a new sentence he leaves *genōh* suspended. Moreover, if *on* were modified to take account of the fragments in the MS. his restoration would be too long, as is Sieper's *þeah þe hē feorran wunie/and mid*. The restorations *feohgestrēona/þæt hē geond* and *þæt hē fēorbūend/geond* illustrate the two main directions in which reconstruction of the text may be sought. The latter serves to underline the contrast between *elþēode*, ' a foreign people ' and *ēþel*, ' a homeland ', in this case by adoption, as in *Genesis* 927, 962.

38-39a. The gap in the text extends to the edge of the MS. page. The tops of three upstrokes appear towards the end of the line. Between the first and second, two or three letters are missing ; between the second and third, one or two letters ; and between the third and the margin, one, or at most two, letters. Between *foldan* and *-ra* in the next line about twenty-two letters altogether are missing. From their spacing, it appears that the last two upstrokes belong to the adjective whose genitive plural ending *-ra* begins the next MS. line. Grein's restoration [*wlonc*]*ra* is untenable because it takes only one of the upstrokes into account. Trautmann (*Anglia*, xvi. 214) restores [*hold*]*ra*, which fits the last two upstrokes and the space available, and allows for a space between *hold-* and the preceding word, which would have ended with a letter containing the first upstroke.

About eighteen letters would then be left to provide the contents of line 38b, which probably contained a verb with an object denoting quantity, upon which *hælepa* and its antecedent adjective depended in the genitive. Grein's contextually suitable restoration *him fela pegniað* is too short. Blackburn's expansion and modification to *fela him þær gehȳrað* (*JGP*, iii. 10) takes no account of the first of the three upstrokes. One modification which would comply with the textual conditions is *him fela pēnian sculon*.

39b-40. Although only the bottom of *e* in *wine* is visible, it can readily be identified from the MS. The gap after *wine* extends to the edge of the MS. page. About seventeen letters are missing. Because Grein's restoration of *dryhten* after *wine* is much too short, Krapp-Dobbie suggests that the line may not have been written out to the edge of the margin. The occasional short lines in the body of a text, however, are never more than two or three letters short of the margin. Shorter lines are confined to the beginnings of texts, after initial letters, when the end of the previous poem has coincided with the end of a line. Trautmann assumes a full line of text missing after *wine* and restores *yrmþe gedreag ā oþþæt hē*, which would be too long even if *þæt* were abbreviated. Blackburn supplements Grein's *dryhten* with *wrǣcca*, inserted at the beginning of line 40a. Although *dryhten wrǣcca* just fills the gap it does not fit into the metrical pattern ; lightly stressed syllables alone are admissible before *nȳde gebǣded*, which already has two major stresses ; cf. *Juliana* 343, *The Metres of Boethius* 6.14. Likewise nothing can be added to line 39b unless *wine* is made to carry the alliteration by restoring an adjective with initial *w* before *hælepa*, a procedure already shown to be untenable. From the foregoing considerations it would appear that a full half-line of text, but not more, is missing after *wine*. Krapp-Dobbie follow many previous editors in their line arrangement :

> . . . . . ra) hæleþa,   þeah þe hēr mīn wine (. . . . .
> nȳde gebǣded   nacan ūt āþrong.

But since no room is metrically available here for the missing text, and since *nȳde gebǣded* is tied to *nacan ūt āþrong* by alliteration, the missing words require to be allotted a line to themselves ; they may have been insufficient to constitute a whole line of poetry, but an isolated half-line is not without precedent, as can be seen from *The Seafarer* 16. One of the missing words was probably the verb in the clause beginning with *þeahþe*, for *áþrong* will not serve since it is in the indicative and a verb in the subjunctive is required, as illustrated in many such clauses in *Beowulf* 682, 1167, 1369, 1927, etc.

42. Only the lower fragments of the word following **ȳþa** are visible. The first and fifth letters can be identified as *g* by their characteristic tails. The second must be a low *e* on account of its low horizontal centre stroke. The third letter is generally held to be *o*, but its first stroke slopes in the wrong direction ; moreover, the fact that it is preceded by a low *e* indicates that it is a letter with an upstroke, for *e* before *o* in this MS. is always of the tall variety forming a ligature. The letter must be *l* or *b*. Hence the frequent reading *geong* first suggested by Trautmann (*Anglia*, xvi. 212-13) must be rejected. For the fourth letter a vowel is required, which may have been *u*, *a*, or *æ*. From the evidence of the fragments, and the necessity for a noun on which *ȳþa* can depend, the word is probably *gelagu*, an alternative suggestion by Trautman ; cf. *The Seafarer*, 64 : *ofer holma gelagu*. After *gelag-* there is space for up to five letters. Ettmüller's restoration *āna* has the merit both of filling the space neatly and of providing, in the second half of line 42, alliteration with *ȳþa* in the first half.

45. **wilna gād** appears to serve two separate genitive constructions : ' he is not lacking in pleasures, in horses . . . nor will he be lacking in any of the treasures of men . . . if he possesses you.' ; cf. *Beowulf* 660, 949-50.

46. The same linking of horses and treasure as the hallmarks of wealth is found in *Maxims* I, 87 and *Beowulf* 2166.

49. Most scholars since Ettmüller have included this line in the preceding sentence, placing a full stop after *twēga*. There has been considerable divergence among them, however, in the interpretation of the preposition *ofer*, which is taken to mean : ' contrary to, against ' by Grein, Bosworth-Toller and Holthausen (*Anglia Beiblatt*, xviii. 207) ; ' after ' by Thorpe and Crawford (*MLR*, xix. 105) ; ' in spite of ' by Gordon, Imelmann and Blackburn (*JGP*, iii. 11) ; ' according to ' by Klaeber (*Archiv*, clxvii. 38-9) and Roeder (*op. cit.* p. 123, n.) ; and ' in addition to ' by Miss Kershaw. The last translation is also adopted by those who, like Trautmann and Mackie, begin a new sentence with *ofer*. This punctuation is supported by the inversion of the verb and its subject in line 50, a procedure usually found after an adverbial phrase such as that comprised by line 49. There is also contextual support for this punctuation ; the *eald gebēot*, none other than the *wordbēotunga* of lines 15-16, is the subject-matter of lines 50-4, with a direct echo of line 16 in line 54. Line 49, therefore, refers not to the man's possession of the woman but the loyalty of the man and woman towards each other. The appropriate interpretation of *ofer* is almost certainly ' concerning ', q.v. B-T, *ofer* II (11), ' denoting the subject of

discourse ' ; cf. the use of the preposition with the same verb *gehȳran* in *Genesis* 17.20 : *ofer Ysmahel ic gehīrde þē*, translating the Latin *super Ismael quoque exaudivi te*, and *Psalm* 118. 162, 1-2 (*Paris Psalter*) : *ic blissige . . . ofer ðīnre sprǣce*, translating *laetabor ego super eloquia tua*.

50. **gehȳre.** Most editors have read *gecyre* here, as if from the verb *gecyrran*. Of those interpreting it as 'turn', Sedgefield takes the verb along with *ǣtsomne* to mean 'rearrange'. Little attention has been paid to Schipper's note (*Germania*, xix. 335) that, scratched and stained as the MS. is at this point, it is *n* or the bottom of *h*, not *c*, which appears faintly in the verb. The transcript clearly supports this reading. The roughening of the parchment, however, is extensive enough for most of the upstroke of an *h* to have disappeared, so that although most of what remains looks like *n*, faint traces of the wedge at the top of *h* confirm the latter reading. Lines 50b and 51 indicate that the verb takes an accusative and infinitive construction, so that the reading *gehȳre* has strong support from the context. Wyatt and Bradley (*MLR*, ii. 367-8) emend to *gehyrde*, unnecessarily, since the present tense for vividness is not unusual.

51. The last rune is somewhat ambiguous and might be read as D, but its similarity in form to the rune in line 23b of *The Ruin*, where it is unambiguously M, supports the reading M here. The meaning of the runes is discussed in the Introduction, pp. 15-17.

53. For the *nn* at the end of **gesprǣconn** instead of the usual single *n* as in line 16, there is a parallel instance in the same MS., in *cwenn* (*Christ* 1198) ; cf. also *gebærann* (*The Fight at Finnsburg* 38), an example which I owe to Dr. K. R. Brooks.

THE RUIN

1-2. Strikingly similar in substance and phrasing are lines 1-3 in *Maxims* II :

> Ceastra bēoð feorran gesȳne,
> orðanc enta geweorc, þā þe on þysse eorðan syndon,
> wrǣtlic weallstāna geweorc.

The use of the phrases *enta geweorc* and *wrǣtlic weallstāna* to amplify *ceastra*, a Latin loan-word used of Roman cities, gives grounds for believing that the same phrases in *The Ruin* may be used of Roman remains also (see A. H. Smith, *English Place-Name Elements*, Part I, p. 85, s.v. *ceaster* (2)). *Enta ǣrgeweorc* refers to the roads within a stone city in *Andreas* 1235, where it is a variant of *wegas* ; cf. also *Andreas* 1495. That stone buildings in England were associated with the Romans is clear from Bede's *Historia Abbatum*, Chap. 5 (edited by C. Plummer, i. 368) where he recounts how Benedict sent to Gaul for stonemasons ' qui lapideam sibi ecclesiam iuxta Romanorum quem semper amabat morem facerent '.

1. Although **þes** is the MS. reading now, there is a space between the first two letters in which faint traces of the left-hand curve of *a*, forming a ligature with *e*, are still visible. An original *þæs* appears to have been emended to *þes* by the deliberate erasure of *a*. Where this word occurs elsewhere in the poem (in lines 9 and 30), the form is *þæs*.

wyrde. Miss Kershaw's personification, ' the Fates ', is unnecessary. The plural form, like the singular, is used elsewhere to refer to ' events ', e.g. *Solomon and Saturn* 334 : *gewurdene wyrda*, where the events, as here, appear to be the hazards liable to be encountered with the passage of time.

2. **burgstede burston.** *Burg*, either alone or compounded, occurs five times in the poem, and has been interpreted both as ' fortified place ' and ' city '. *Burgstede*, however, always has reference to the latter ; cf. the same phrase in *Christ* 811, also *Guthlac* 1317 and *Bwf.* 2265 ' court '.

4. **hrungeat berofen.** Most editors are agreed that the MS. reading *hrim geat torras berofen* is corrupt. The omission of *torras*, assumed to have been inadvertently repeated from the previous line, gives a metrically complete half-line. But, since *hrim* makes no sense here, and also occurs in the second half-line, it is probable that this word too is corrupt. Grein proposed (*Germania*, x. 422) the emendation of *hrim geat* to *hrungeat*, for *hrunggeat* ' spar-gate ', with simplification of *gg*. Both Sieper's *hrumge berofene* and Kock's *hrunge berofene* (*Anglia*, xlvi. 178-9) involve considerable emendation, whereas Grein's reading is palaeographically sounder, assuming no more than the common error, by the copyist of the MS., of misreading four strokes and writing *im* for *un*.

5. **scŭrbeorge,** ' protections against storms ', occurs only here, and is usually interpreted as a figurative expression for ' roofs '. But roofs have already been mentioned in the same sentence (3), and the position of *scŭrbeorge*, at the end of the list which begins with *hrōfas*, makes it unlikely that it is a variant of the latter. It may be that, as Schücking suggests in the glossary to his edition, the compound is used by metonymy for buildings. Some support for the basic meaning ' roofs ' is forthcoming from a similar compound in *Genesis* 813, where Adam and Eve complain that they have no *scŭrsceade* against the hail, frost and hot sunshine from the heavens.

6. **undereotone.** The rare *-on-* inflexion of the past participle can be paralleled from the same stem in *þurhetone* (*Beowulf* 3049) ; cf. also Sievers-Brunner, § 366, Anm. 3 and 4. The back mutation of *e* to *eo* can be paralleled in the preterite plural *ēoton* (Peterborough version of *The Anglo-Saxon Chronicle*, 998), in place of the more regular *ēton* ; cf. also Sievers-Brunner, § 370 and Anm. 1.

7. **waldendwyrhtan.** Ettmüller and other early editors interpreted MS. *waldend wyrhtan* as elements of a compound noun. Krapp-Dobbie objects that such a compound would be highly unusual and takes the words as separate nouns with asyndetic parataxis. Miss Von Schaubert (' Zur Erklärung Schwierigkeiten bietender altenglischer Textstellen ', *Philologica, Malone Anniversary Studies*, p. 38) claims that both these unsatisfactory courses are obviated by placing a comma after *waldend* and taking *wyrhtan* and the two following participles as a nominative absolute construction which will lead on naturally to the next sentence : ' earth's grip holds the rulers, the builders being dead, departed.' The abrupt transition from rulers to builders, however, is a *non sequitur*. Support for an *ad hoc* compound *waldendwyrhtan* can be found in poetic compounds of a similar type, such as *āgendfrēa, winedryhten* and *frēawine*. Compounds of this type appear to have been much more common in the earlier history of the Germanic languages ; see C. T. Carr, *Nominal Compounds in Germanic* (Oxford 1939), pp. xxvi, 328-9.

forweorone is the inflected form of the past participle of the infinitive *forweosan* ' to pass away ', according to Sievers-Brunner (§ 382, Anm. 3). The regular past participle is *forweren* (see J. E. Cross, ' On Sievers-Brunner's Interpretation of *The Ruin* 7, " *Forweorone Geleorene* " ', *English and Germanic Studies*, vi (1957), 105 and n. 6). Sievers-Brunner takes what he calls the MS. form *forweoren* as a scribal error for *forworen*, with *o* by analogy with strong verbs of Class IV. The MS. form, however, is *forweorone* with *-on-* as the participial inflexion, as in several presumed early and Anglian forms ; see Sievers-Brunner, § 366, Anm. 3. If back mutation did not occur in the past participle, *eo* may have been transferred by analogy from the preterite plural ; cf. Sievers-Brunner, § 378, Anm. 3.

geleorene. The verb *lēoran* is generally conjugated weak, but a past participle of a Class II strong verb occurs as *loren* in Wærferð's translation of Gregory's *Dialogues* edited by H. Hecht, *Bibliothek der angelsäch-sischen Prosa*, v. 286, line 24. Bertil Weman lists the past participle *geleorene* under *geleoran* (*Old English Semantic Analysis and Theory* (Lund 1933), p. 74) which he states is used euphemistically of human beings, meaning ' to die '. The *eo* of the stem, in place of the expected *o* as in *loren*, may be due to corruption under the influence of *forweorone*, as suggested by Sievers-Brunner, § 384, Anm. 3 ; but the rhyme appears to be deliberate, as in line 5, and *geleorene* may be a genuine form, with analogical diphthong from the present, the analogy being assisted by the existence of the much more common weak form *geléored*.

8. **cnēa.** This is an unusual form of the genitive plural of the neuter noun *cnēo*, ' generation '. A parallel form *trēa*, genitive plural of *trēo* ' tree ', occurs in the *Vespasian Psalter* 73.5. Cf. Sievers-Brunner, § 250, Anm. 4, and Campbell, § 278-80.

8-9. ' until . . . [shall] have passed away '. I agree with Bruce Mitchell, *Neophilologus*, xlix (1965), 44-6, as to the meaning of this clause. In the light of his comments, however, I abandon my former interpretation of MS. *gewitan* as an infinitive with *sculon* understood to indicate futurity, and revert to the usual interpretation of *gewitan* as preterite indicative : cf. Mitchell's illustrations of the use of the present and past indicative in *oppæt* clauses in *Phoenix* 151-2 and *Christ* 1005-6.

10. **ræghār.** The first element of this compound adjective was frequently derived from *rǣge*, ' she-goat ', as in Grein-Köhler and Bosworth-Toller. But besides providing an incongruous poetic image here, such a derivation is not in accord with the relationship between elements seen in the similarly formed adjective *feaxhār*, ' grey-haired ' ; if the first element is taken as from *ragu*, ' lichen ', as by Miss Kershaw and Mackie, then by analogy with *feaxhār* the compound will mean ' grey with lichen '.

rēadfāh, according to Earle (*Proceedings of the Bath Natural History and Antiquities Field Club*, ii. 269), describes the stains on the stones made by iron oxide from the springs at Bath. Miss Kershaw maintains that it refers to the prevailing colour of the internal walls, of bricks, mortar and especially of the red plaster, much of which still adheres to the walls of the great bath-house today. But *rēadfāh* is linked with *ræghār*, and it is difficult to conceive that the poet is thinking simultaneously of the outside and inside walls. Moreover, the meaning of *fāh* is not very appropriate for the description of smooth expanses of red plaster. The association with *ræghār* and the dappled or variegated effects associated with *fāh* are satisfied by taking the adjective to refer to the orange-tinted lichen of Bath, variegated with the grey variety.

11. **gēap** is taken as a noun by Miss Kershaw, who finds support for it in the gloss of L. *cornas* as *gēap* in *Anglo-Saxon and Old English Vocabularies*, edited by T. Wright and R. P. Wülcker, i. 274.4 ; but the glossary list which includes *cornas* is otherwise solely of animals, and it is highly probable that the Latin was originally *coruus*, ' crow ',

misread at some stage in transmission as *curuus*, ' curved ', and then
corrupted to *cornas*. Support for *gēap* as an adjective meaning ' curved,
bent, arched ' is, on the other hand, plentiful in the same collection ;
cf. the glosses *curfa* 377.37, *pando* 486.9 and for *gēapum, pandis* 37.17,
curuis 377.7. As in *The Ruin*, the adjectives *stēap* and *gēap* appear in
the same context on a number of occasions in Old English poetry, as in
Maxims II 23, *Solomon and Saturn* 415, *Genesis* 2558. If *gēap* is an
adjective like *stēap*, it must refer to the *wāg* ' wall ' (9). In *Solomon
and Saturn* 257, *gēap* also refers to a wall, and must mean ' curved ',
because the wall is a mountain surrounding the bird referred to in lines
255 and 256. In *The Ruin* reference may be either to a wall with part
of an arch remaining, or to the curved wall of a tower, for *torras* are
mentioned in line 3. The *Ruin* poet has a penchant for asyndetic
parataxis ; here *stēap gēap* corresponds to the co-ordinate expression
stēap ond gēap found wherever these two adjectives occur together
elsewhere in Old English ; cf. lines 5, 7, 35 and 36 for other examples
of the omission of the co-ordinate conjunction.

12. The *e* of *se-* cannot be the final letter of the word because,
although incomplete, it has the loop of tall *e*, which is always followed
immediately by a small letter in this MS. Since a noun appears to
have been lost in the gap which follows, an *o* forming a ligature with *e*
is probably to be restored, giving *sēo*, the nominative feminine singular
of the definite article preceding the lost noun.

The word ending in *-rum* in the second half-line was probably a
noun depending in the dative on *gehēawen* and beginning with *w* to
alliterate with *wōrað* in the first half-line ; the emphatic position of
wōrað indicates that it may have carried the alliteration, along with the
noun after *sēo*, giving double alliteration as in most first half-lines in
the poem.

Almost all editors have accepted Ettmüller's emendation of MS.
geheapen to *geheawen*. The Old English verb *geheapian* is weak and
the past participle is always *geheapod*. Confusion of *p* and *w* is not
infrequent because of the similarity in form of the OE letters.

A possible restoration of the whole line is :

wōrað gīet sēo winburg   wederum gehēawen.

13. The first word **fēlon** is probably the Mercian form of the pre-
terite plural of *fēolan*, from **feolhan*, a strong verb of Class III, which,
with loss of intervocalic *h*, often went over into Class IV, giving WS
fǣlon, and Mercian *fēlun* as in the *Vespasian Psalter* ; cf. Sievers-
Brunner, § 387, Anm. 2.

With reference to the letter beyond the gap, the MS. shows clearly,
as the facsimile does not, the distinctive top hook of a low *e*. There is
no trace of the letter in the transcript.

15. Since *heo* comes at the end of a line in the MS., and the gap

extends from the margin in the following line, it is uncertain whether *heo* is the nominative of the feminine pronoun or the first part of a longer word such as *heolde*, which was completed at the beginning of the next line in the MS.

16. After **g** and before **orþonc,** Mackie claims that there is the merest trace of the foot of a small letter. From the facsimile this might be dismissed as a mark on the vellum, but the MS. shows it to be in ink ; nevertheless, it is too small to have formed part of any letter, for enough of the vellum remains intact in its vicinity to make it certain that more would have been visible had the ink mark been intended as part of a letter.

Sieper puts *orþonc ǣrsceaft* together in the first half of line 16, Mackie in the second half ; but the size of the gaps which precede and follow the two words makes the former arrangement highly unlikely. Sieper's allowance of two complete half-lines of verse for the gap between *ǣrsceaft* and *lāmrindum* is too generous. Mackie's procedure makes adequate allowance for the difference in the size of the gaps but gives two alliterating syllables in a second half-line, a most unlikely feature. Both *orþonc,* as in *Maxims* II 2, and *ǣr-* compounds, like *ǣrgewyrhtu* in *Christ* 1240b, carry alliteration. *Orþonc* must therefore be put in the first and *ǣrsceaft* in the second half-line, an arrangement which makes it probable that *orþonc* is the noun ' skill ', not an adjective as indicated in Bosworth-Toller and Grein-Köhler. The missing word ending in *-g* which precedes it is consequently likely to have been an adjective qualifying *orþonc.*

17. Between **g** and **lamrindum** in the facsimile there is what appears to be the bottom curve of a small letter, which Mackie thinks might be *e*. However, when the MS. folio is held to the light, it can be clearly seen to be part of a letter showing through from the other side, a fragment of *b* in line 12 of folio 124b.

Lāmrindum is a unique compound from whose elements we may deduce the meaning ' rinds or crusts of earth or clay '. Perhaps it refers to the silt or mud stirred up by the actions of the hot springs and encrusting the ruined buildings. The position of *bēag* at the end of the line makes it likely that it is the 3 singular preterite indicative of *būgan,* ' to bend '. The subject is probably one of the ruins, for instance the *ǣrsceaft* of line 16, which sank beneath encrustations of mud, *lāmrindum* being in the instrumental case after *bēag.*

18. **Mod mo-** comes at the end of a MS. line, and the first few letters of the following line are missing. Few words beginning with *mo-*, of six to eight letters altogether, could fit the context ; a verb appears to be required, probably *monade* meaning ' instigated ', as in *monað mōdes lust* in *The Seafarer* 36 ; for the syntax of the line, cf. *mōd mǣgnade mine fǣgnade* in *The Rhyming Poem* 33. *Gebregdan* is usually found with concrete objects in Old English ; the basic meaning of quick movement, as exemplified in the noun *gebregd* in *Phoenix* 57, is probably

intended here ; cf. Mackie's 'made active'. The whole line might then be translated as 'the mind suggested, stimulated a swift purpose '.

20. **weallwalan.** Grein drew attention to the parallel compound *wyrtwalan*, glossing Latin *radices*, ' roots ', which throws light on the word and suggests the meaning ' foundations of walls '.

wīrum. The other Old English contexts in which this word appears are confined to decoration, usually of filigree in metal, and there are no parallels for its obviously functional purpose here. Miss Kershaw suggests that it refers to the iron rods or cramps with which Roman foundations were often held together. Professor Richmond has found abundant evidence on the stonework at Bath for the use of cramps, both in the baths and in the temple of Sul Minerva. The binding of stones into circles could refer either to the bases of columns or the *torras* referred to in line 3.

21. **burnsele** does not occur elsewhere, although its elements are common and indicate clearly ' halls with running water ', i.e. ' bathing halls '. Lines 38-41 support this interpretation.

22. **horngestrēon** is frequently translated as ' a wealth of pinnacles ', but where Old English glosses for *pinnaculum* occur they are compounds of *horn* such as *hornpīc* and *hornscēaða*. Referring to buildings by itself in Old English, *horn* appears to mean ' gable projections curved like horns ' as in *Andreas* 668, *Beowulf* 82, 704. Since *gestrēon* indicates nothing more than a large number of *hornas* the translation of *hēah horngestrēon* is ' a profusion of lofty gables '; cf. *Riddle* 3.63.

23. **mondrēama.** Here as in *The Husband's Message* 50, the runic letter before *dreama* in the MS. could be interpreted from its form alone either as *M* or *D*. The alliteration, however, requires that it shall be *M*, in which case it is an abbreviation for *monn*, part of the compound *mondrēama*, ' joys of men ', which occurs several times elsewhere in Old English poetry, and in the place-name Mondrum in Cheshire.

24. **wyrd sēo swīþe.** This same phrase occurs in *Solomon and Saturn* 444, where, as Lumiansky has noted (*Neophilologus*, xxvi. 25), it is a deliberate pre-Christian use, as the context makes clear. *Wyrd* is the subject of *onwende*, whose object is *þæt*, i.e. the state of affairs referred to in lines 21-3. The concept of this line is similar to that in *The Wanderer* 107 : *onwendeð wyrda . gesceaft weoruld under heofonum.*

26. **secgrōfra wera.** Many editors have retained MS. *secg rof* with the sense ' host of men ', in support of which meaning Toller, in his *Anglo-Saxon Dictionary Supplement* under *stæfrōf*, cites the latter compound which glossed Latin *elementum*, ' the letters of the alphabet ' (*Anglo-Saxon and Old English Vocabularies*, i. 397.14). Under *secgrōf* Bosworth-Toller cites OHG *ruoba* (f.) in support of the meaning 'number' for *-rōf* ; the latter must, however, be neuter in Old English in order that *eall* should agree with it. More formidable objections arise to the interpretation of *secg* as ' man ' ; although this word can mean ' sedge ',

interpretation of *secg* as ' man ' ; although this word can mean ' sedge ',
' man ', or ' sea ' in Old English, as the first element of a compound
it is found only with the meaning ' sword '. If -*rōf* is taken as the
adjective ' brave, valiant ', then *secg* must mean ' sword ', for *rōf* is
always compounded with inanimate objects. Emended to *secgrōfra* to
agree with *wera*, the adjective, meaning ' sword-valiant ', is parallel in
formation to *æscrōf* (*Judith* 12).

27. **wigsteal** is generally taken as a compound of *wīg* ' war ' and
steall ' place ', which occurs twice elsewhere, in *Solomon and Saturn*
103 and *Vainglory* 39. Mackie suggests (*MLN*, xl. 92) taking *wīg* as
' idol ' and *wigsteal* as ' place of idols, temple ', the whole line comprising
a reminiscence of Amos vii. 9 : ' et demolientur excelsa idoli, et sancti-
ficationes Israel desolabuntur.' A form *weocsteall* is found glossing
Latin *absida* (see *ES*, xi. 64), and *weohstealle* appears in the Laws of
Edgar, but these appear to be variant forms of *wīgbed* or *weofod*, ' idol '.
All the many other compounds of *wīg* in Old English are used in the
context of war.

28. **bētend** refers to those who should have repaired the *burgsteall*
' city ', which *brosnade*, ' crumbled away '. Compare the similarity
of vocabulary in *Christ* 13 : *ond þonne gebēte, nū gebrosnad is*/*hūs under
hrōfe*, an image of the Lord as the builder and rebuilder of a house
elaborated in the context. Other similarities between the two poems
are *weallstān* in *The Ruin* 1 and *Christ* 2, *waldendwyrhtan* in *The Ruin* 7
and *wyrhtan* in *Christ* 2.

· 30. **þæs tēaforgēapa.** Early editors take -*gēapa* as a noun, ' arch,
gable ', and so Mackie and Mossé, who put a comma after it, making it a
subject of *drēorgiað* like *hofu*. Kirkland (*AJP*, vii. 368) assumes a
weak noun *geapa* ; although he cites OHG *goufana*, ' cupped hand ' as
a possible cognate, and Hoops gives OLG *gōpa*, ON *gaupn* and other
medieval Germanic forms from the same root (*ES*, lxiv. 202), these are
all feminine, and a noun *geapa* would have to be masculine here ;
moreover, there is no indication in Old English glosses for parts of the
body of a similar cognate for ' cupped hand ', which is simply *hōl
hand* ; *s.v.* Bosworth-Toller, *hōl*. It is more likely that *gēapa* is the
weak form of the adjective *gēap*, ' curved ', discussed in the note to
line 11. Krapp-Dobbie's objection is that if it is an adjective we
should expect the form *gēapan* to agree with *hrostbēages* ; but it can very
well qualify *hrōf*, which is masculine and nominative as *þæs* and *tēa-
forgēapa* require.

The first element *tēafor* is generally taken to be the noun which
glosses Latin *minium*, ' vermilion ' in *Anglo-Saxon and Old English
Vocabularies*, i. 314.21 ; cf. ON *taufr* with the same meaning. There is
some doubt whether in fact the Anglo-Saxons meant by *tēafor*, ' cinna-
bar ', the red mercury sulphide from which vermilion is extracted. It
may have denoted any mineral from which red pigment was obtained,
such as iron oxide, *q.v.* M. Förster, *Anglia Beiblatt*, xxxiv. 100-4.

However, the common element in all the uses of the word is undoubtedly a reddish colour.

31. hróstbéages hróf. Early editors, and more recently Sieper and Mackie, have kept the MS. *hrost beages rof*, the latter translating it ' the roofwork strong and circular '. But *róf* cannot be an adjective in this context for it always refers to a personal quality, ' brave, valiant '. Grein (*Germania*, x. 422) emended to *hróf*. Two alliterating syllables are the rule in first half-lines in this poem, so that it is probable that *róf* is a scribal form for earlier *hróf* at a time when *h* before *l* and *r* was disappearing ; cf. Sievers-Brunner, § 217, Anm. 2.

Hróst occurs once elsewhere in Old English, with the meaning ' hen-roost '. Kirkland (*AJP*, vii. 369) drew attention to its occurrence in the Old Saxon *Heliand* 70.23 as ' roof ', a meaning also to be found in Scots dialect. But Bosworth-Toller shows that its use in Scots is more specifically of the frame of the inner roof. Furthermore, the Biblical context of *The Heliand* makes clear that the inner roof is meant, for Christ inside the house saw the sick man being lowered *thurh thes húses hróst*.

Béag in Old English is usually associated with money or circular ornaments, but a more general meaning ' circle ' is found in *béahhyrne*, ' corner of the eye ', *v.* Toller *béah* (4). Here compounded with *hróst* it must mean ' of the circle formed by the inner framework of the roof '. In lines 30-1 the poet appears to be saying that the red curved roof—of the circle formed by the inner roof—parts from its tiles. Box tiles were often used by the Romans in the construction of ceilings in order to lessen the weight of vaults and domes. Extensive roofage of this kind was found at Bath, in the Great Bath.

hryre wong gecrong. Beginning a new sentence with line 31, Grein-Köhler (*hryre*, p. 362) takes *hróstbéages hróf* as the subject of *gecrong*, *wong* as an accusative, and *hryre* as instrumental singular. *Gecringan* is generally intransitive, as in the similar context in *Beowulf* 1568, *héo on flet gecrong* ; however, the synonymous verb *gefeallan* takes a direct object when used perfectively, ' to gain the land by falling '. Exactly parallel to this passage in syntax and metre is *lagu land geféol* (*Exodus* 483), ' water fell on land ', as pointed out to me by J. E. Cross.

32. tó beorgum. The preposition here may be taken with *gecrong* to indicate that the *hryre*, ' ruin ', fell upon existing heaps of rubble, or with *gebrocen* to denote a change of condition, as indicated by Bosworth-Toller, *s.v.* *tó* 2(a), p. 990, in which case the meaning is that the ruin fell, broken into heaps of stone.

33. gleoma gefrætwed. Grein suggested emendation to *gleoman* as from a weak noun *glimu/gleoma* related to *glǽm*. More recent editors generally keep *gleoma* as genitive plural of a noun *gleomu* (f.) ' splendour ' (*q.v.* Grein-Köhler, *gleomu*, *glimu*, p. 267), used adverbially. But genitive plurals used adverbially are few and mainly of relatively colourless nouns like *þing* and *geár* (see Campbell, § 666). An instrumental case is required here; cf. *hyrstum frætwed* (*Riddles* 14.11, 31.20), *gimmum gefrætewod* (*Christ and Satan* 647), *fiðrum gefrætwad* (*Elene* 742, *Phoenix* 239). It is more likely, therefore, that *gleoma* is the instrumental of a *u* stem noun *gleomu*.

34. **wlonc ond wingāl,** ' proud and flushed with wine '. The same phrase occurs in *The Seafarer* 29. The only other occurrence of *wingāl* is in *Daniel* 116.

36. **eorcanstān.** As Cross points out (*Neophilologus*, xxxix. 204-5) translators have overlooked the oddity of the singular form here. No special jewel is mentioned, and in this generalised passage the plural is expected, as in *searogimmas* in line 35; cf. *Elene* 1023-4. Cross's solution, that it is parallel to *þās beorhtan burg* in line 37, is syntactically attractive but semantically doubtful. His prose citations of figurative uses of the word (p. 205, n. 6) are in all cases faithful translations of the Latin *margarita*. There is no instance to justify the assumption that *eorcanstān* in Old English could mean anything other than precious stone, usually either topaz or pearl. Moreover, the series of objects of *seah* (35) with the preposition *on* is cumulative; there is no distinctive linkage between *eorcanstān* and *burg*, such as *ond* after *æht* would have provided, to mark these nouns off as appositional. The singular form is probably to be interpreted collectively as jewellery, as the similar compound *sincstān* in *Metres of Boethius* 21.21. The first element of the compound is common to other Germanic languages; cf. OHG *erchan*, ' egregius, summus ', Gothic *aírkns*, ON *jarknasteinn*. It is derived ultimately from Chaldean *jarkan*, ' topaz ', through Greek and Latin.

38. **hāte** cannot be an adverb ' hotly ', since *weorpan* is never used intransitively without a following preposition. The form must therefore be the dative singular of the noun *hāt*, the dative of the thing thrown, after *wearp*; cf. *beorges weard ... wearp wælfȳre* (*Beowulf* 2582).

41. **hāt on hreþre.** The same phrase occurs in *Beowulf* 3148 and *Christ and Satan* 98, where it refers to the heat generated internally by the funeral fire and a dragon respectively. That the heat of the water in the baths was self-generated is a clear indication of the presence of the thermal springs, suggested by lines 38-9.

hȳpelic, ' convenient ', probably in relation to the arrangements for utilising the hot water. Metrically this half-line is defective. Holthausen (*Anglia Beiblatt*, xlvi. 10) would add *þing* by analogy with line 48b; cf. also *Riddle* 39.24 : *þæt is wrǣtlic þing*.

42. Here the damage to the MS. again begins to affect the text of the poem. Of the word after *gēotan* only the upstroke of the initial letter remains. Mackie states that it is perhaps part of *l*, but the trace of a curve attached to it indicates that it is *þ*.

45. The MS. *oþþæt* can be taken either as a conjunction ' until ' introducing a subordinate clause, or as the preposition *oþ*, ' up to ' followed by the neuter singular accusative of the demonstrative

adjective *þæt*, qualifying *hringmere*.   Since *hāte*, and not a verb, follows
hringmere, the latter interpretation is preferable.

hringmere may refer to the circular bath at Bath excavated in 1885,
as suggested by Miss Kershaw.   The compound occurs nowhere else
in Old English, although its elements are common.   Herben (*MLN*,
lix. 73) suggests that it is a kenning, but it fits the context better if
taken as a straightforward descriptive compound, as in the place-name
Ringmer in Sussex.

The first of the fragments after *hāte* has a downstroke peculiar to
the form of *s* which immediately precedes *t* in this MS.   Krapp-Dobbie
conjectures that the word which these fragments begin may have been
strēamas, although the phrase *hāte strēamas* occurs only two lines above
(43).   There is support for repetition in this passage, however, for
line 46b repeats 40b.

47. There are marks in the facsimile beyond *is*.   These Mackie
takes to be part of the next word, but they are seen from the MS. to
be a part of *g* showing through from the other side of the folio.

49. The noun *hūse* is improbable after *þing* (48) ; but if *sē* is taken
as the article qualifying a noun lost in the gap, and *hū* is taken as a
conjunction, then line 49 begins with a clause explanatory of the
demonstrative pronoun *þæt* in the main clause in line 48.

Possibly at least two of the last three spaces in the last short MS.
line were taken up by the usual sign indicating the end of a poem.   By
reason of their length and spacing the two downstrokes beyond *burg*
appear to belong to a looped *s* and an *r* occurring in the group *str*.

GLOSSARY

The Glossary is intended to include all occurrences of all forms in the texts. The order of words is strictly alphabetical ; æ follows **ad, þ** and **ð** are treated as one letter and follow **t**, the words prefixed by **ge-** follow **gēap**. The gender of nouns is indicated by the abbreviations *m., f., n. (noun* is implied). The numbers after *sv.* and *wv.* refer to the classes of strong and weak verbs respectively, as indicated in Campbell's *Old English Grammar*. The line references to restored or emended forms are italicised.

ā *adv.* continually WL 5, always WL 42.

ābīdan *sv.* 1 to await WL 53.

āctrēo *n.* oak tree ; *dat. sg.* WL 28, 36.

ādrāf *see* **ādrīfan**.

ādrīfan *sv.* 1 to drive away ; *3 sg. pret.* **ādrāf** HM 19.

ǣfre *adv.* ever WL 39.

æfter *prep. w. dat.* after R 10.

ǣht *f.* property ; *acc. sg.* R 36.

ælde *m. pl.* men ; *gen. pl.* **ælda** *HM 3*.

ældo *f.* age ; *dat. sg.* R 6.

ǣnig *pron.* any ; *gen. sg. n.* **ǣnges** HM 47.

ǣrdæg *m.* former day ; *dat. pl.* **ǣrdagum** HM 16, 54.

ǣrest *adv. superl.* first WL 6.

ǣrsceaft *n.* ancient work ; *nom. sg.* R 16.

æt *prep. w. dat.* to WL 45.

ætsomne *adv.* together HM 33, 50.

āgrafan *sv.* 6 to inscribe ; *3 sg. pret.* **āgrōf** HM 13.

āgrōf *see* **āgrafan**.

āh *v.* I possess ; *1 sg. pret.* **āhte** WL 16.

alwaldend *adj.* almighty ; *nom. sg. m.* HM 32.

ān *adj.* one ; *acc. sg. n.* HM 18 ; *wk. nom. sg. m.* **āna** alone WL 22, *HM 42, wk. nom. sg. f.* WL 35.

āþ *m.* oath ; *dat. sg.* **āþe** HM 51.

āþringan *sv.* 3 to push out ; *3 sg. pret.* **āþrong** HM 41.

āþrong *see* **āþringan**.

āweaxan *sv.* 7 to grow up ; *1 sg. pret.* **āwēox** *WL 3*, HM 2.

āwēox *see* **āweaxan**.

bæþ *n.* bath ; *nom. pl.* **baþu** R 40, 46.

bāt *m.* boat ; *gen. sg.* **bātes** HM 6.

baþu *see* **bæþ**.

be *prep. w. dat.* concerning, touching HM 53.

bēag *see* **būgan**.

bēag *m.* bracelet ; *acc. pl.* **bēagas** HM 35.

bēam *m.* tree ; *acc. sg.* HM 13.

bearu *m.* grove ; *dat. sg.* **bearwe** WL 27, HM 23.

befēng *see* **befōn**.

beflōwan *sv.* 7 to maroon ; *pp.* **beflōwen** WL 49.

befōn *sv.* 7 to enclose ; *3 sg. pret.* **befēng** R 39.

begeat *see* **begietan**.

begietan *sv.* 5 to lay hold on ; *3 sg. pret.* **begeat** WL 32, 41.

behriman *wv.* 1 to cover with rime ; *pp.* **behrimed** WL 48.

beneah *v.* I possess ; *3 sg. pres.* HM 48.

benemnan *wv.* 1 to declare ; HM 51.

beorg *m.* mound of stone ; *dat. pl.*
beorgum R 32.

beorht *adj.* bright ; *nom. pl. n.* R
21 ; *wk. acc. sg. f.* beorhtan R
37, *wk. dat. sg. m.* R 40.

beorn *m.* warrior ; *nom. sg.* R 32.

bēotian *wv.* 2 to vow ; 1 *pl. pret.*
bēotedan WL 21.

berēofan *sv.* 2 to destroy ; *pp.*
berofen R 4.

berofen *see* berēofan.

berstan *sv.* 3 to fall apart ; 3 *pl.
pret.* burston R 2.

bētend *m.* rebuilder ; *nom. pl.* R 28.

beweaxan *sv.* 7 to grow over ; *pp.
nom. pl. m.* beweaxne WL 31.

bī *prep. w. dat.* about WL 1.

biddan *sv.* 5 to beseech HM 13.

biter *adj.* sharp ; *nom. pl. m.*
bitre WL 31.

bið *see* wesan.

blīþe *adj.* cheerful ; *acc. sg. n.* WL
44, *instr. sg. n.* WL 21.

bōsm *m.* bosom ; *dat. sg.* bōsme
HM 6, R 40.

brād *adj.* broad ; *wk. gen. sg. n.*
brādan R 37.

brēostcearu *f.* grief of heart ; *acc.
sg.* brēostceare WL 44.

brēr *m.* briar ; *dat. pl.* brērum WL
31.

brosnian *wv.* 2 to decay ; 3 *sg.
pres.* brosnað R 2, 3 *sg. pret.*
brosnade R 28.

brytnian *wv.* 2 to distribute *HM 34.*

būgan *sv.* 2 to bend ; 3 *sg. pret.*
bēag R 17.

būgan *wv.* 3 to inhabit HM 18.

burg *f.* city ; *acc. sg.* R 37, *case
unknown* R 49.

burgrǣced *n.* city hall ; *nom. pl.*
R 21.

burgsteall *n.* city ; *nom. sg.* R 28.

burgstede *m.* city building ; *nom.
pl.* R 2.

burgtūn *m.* protecting hedge ; *nom.
pl.* burgtūnas WL 31.

burnsele *m.* bathing hall ; *nom. pl.*
R 21.

burston *see* berstan.

cēolþelu *f.* ship ; *dat. sg.* cēolþele
HM 9.

cnēo *n.* generation : *gen. pl.* cnēa
R 8.

cringan *sv.* 3 to fall ; 3 *pl. pret.*
crungon R 25, 28.

cuman *sv.* 4 to come ; 3 *pl. pret.*
cwōman R 25, *pp.* cumen HM 8.

cunnan *v.* to know HM 9.

cwōman *see* cuman.

cynelic *adj.* noble ; *nom. sg. n.*
R 48.

dæg *m.* day ; *acc. sg.* WL 37.

dear *v.* I dare ; 1 *sg. pres.* HM 11.

dēað *m.* death ; *nom. sg.* WL 22.

denu *f.* valley ; *nom. pl.* dena WL
30.

dim *adj.* gloomy ; *nom. pl. f.*
dimme WL 30.

dohtor *f.* daughter ; *gen. sg.* HM
48.

drēfan *wv.* 1 to stir ; 2 *sg. pret.
subj.* drēfde HM 21.

drēogan *sv.* 2 to suffer WL 26 ;
3 *sg. pres.* drēogeð WL 50.

drēorgian *wv.* 2 to grow desolate ;
3 *pl. pres.* drēorgiað R 29.

drēorsele *m.* desolate hall ; *dat. sg.*
WL 50.

dūn *f.* hill ; *nom. pl.* dūna WL 30.

dyrne *adj.* secret ; *acc. sg. m.* WL
12.

ēac þon *adv.* moreover, besides WL
44.

ēad *n.* wealth ; *acc. sg.* R 36.

eal *adv.* completely WL 29.

eald *adj.* ancient ; *nom. sg. m.* WL
29, *acc. sg. n.* HM 49.

ealdes *adv.* long ago WL 4.

eall *adj.* all ; *gen. sg. m.* ealles WL
41, *nom. sg. f.* eal WL 46 ; *pron.
acc. sg. n.* eall R 26, 39.

eard *m.* abode ; *acc. sg. WL 15,*
HM 18.

earfoð *n.* hardship ; *gen. pl.* earfoða
WL 39.

eft *adv.* back WL 23.

elles *adv.* else WL 23.

ellor *adv.* elsewhere HM 4.

elþēod *f.* foreign people ; *acc. sg.* elþēode HM 37.

ent *m.* giant ; *gen. pl.* enta R 2.

eom *see* wesan.

eorcanstān *m.* jewellery ; *acc. sg.* R 36.

eorlgestrēon *n.* noble treasure ; *gen. pl.* eorlgestrēona HM 47.

eorþe *f.* earth ; *dat. sg.* eorþan WL 33, HM 47.

eorðgrāp *f.* grip of earth; *nom. sg.* R 6.

eorðscræf *n.* cave ; *dat. sg.* eorðscræfe WL 28, *acc. pl.* eorðscrafu WL 36.

eorðsele *m.* cave, barrow ; *nom. sg.* WL 29.

ēþel *m.* domain ; *acc. sg.* HM 26, 37.

fǣdan *see* fǣgan.

fǣgan *wv.* 1 to burnish ; *pp. gen. sg. n.* fǣdan HM 36.

fæger *adj.* fair ; *acc. sg. f.* fægre HM 38.

fǣhðu *f.* feud ; *nom. sg.* fǣhþo HM 19, *acc. sg.* fǣhðu WL 26.

fāh *adj.* outcast ; *nom. sg. m.* WL 46.

faran *sv.* 6 to voyage HM 43.

fela *adj. indecl. w. gen. pl.* many WL 39.

felalēof *adj.* dearly loved ; *wk. gen. sg. m.* felalēofan WL 26.

fēlon *see* fēolan.

fēolan *sv.* 4 to penetrate ; 3 *pl. pret.* fēlon R 13.

feor *adv.* far WL 25.

feorr *adj.* far ; *gen. sg. n.* feorres WL 47.

fēran *wv.* 1 to journey WL 9.

findan *sv.* 3 to find ; 2 *sg. pres.* findest HM 12, 28, 1 *sg. pret.* funde WL 18.

flotweg *m.* sea ; *acc. sg.* HM 43.

folclond *n.* country ; *gen. sg.* folclondes WL 47.

folde *f.* earth ; *acc. sg.* foldan *HM 38.*

folgað *m.* service ; *acc. sg.* WL 9.

for *prep. w. dat.* because of WL 10.

forniman *sv.* 4 to take away ; 3 *sg. pret.* fornōm R 26 ; *pp.* fornumen *WL 24.*

fornōm *see* forniman.

forþon *adv.* therefore WL 17, R 29 ; *conj.* because WL 39.

forðsīþ *m.* departure ; *gen. sg.* forðsīþes HM 43.

forweorone *see* forweosan.

forweosan *sv.* 1 to perish ; *pp. acc. pl.* forweorone R 7.

frēa *m.* lord ; *gen. sg.* frēan WL 33, HM 10.

fremman *wv.* 1 to display HM 19.

frēond *m.* friend, lover ; *nom. sg.* WL 47, *nom. pl.* frȳnd WL 33, *gen. pl.* frēonda WL 17.

frēondscipe *m.* love ; *nom. sg.* WL 25, *acc. sg.* frēondscype HM 19.

fromsīþ *m.* departure ; *nom. sg.* WL 33.

frȳnd *see* frēond.

ful *adv.* most WL 1, 18 ; very WL 21, 32, 46, HM 6.

full *adj.* filled ; *nom. sg. f.* R 23.

funde *see* findan.

gād *n.* lack ; *nom. sg.* HM 45.

galan *sv.* 6 to sing HM 23.

ge *conj.* and WL 25.

gēac *m.* cuckoo ; *acc. sg.* HM 23.

geador *adv.* together HM 50.

geann *v.* I grant ; 3 *sg. pres. subj.* geunne HM 32.

gēap *adj.* curved ; *nom. sg. m.* R 11.

gebād *see* gebīdan.

gebǣdan *wv.* 1 to compel ; *pp.* gebǣded HM 41.

gebǣro *n.* demeanour ; *acc. sg.* WL 44, *instr. sg.* WL 21.

gebēot *n.* promise ; *acc. sg.* HM 49.

gebīdan *sv.* 1 to experience ; 1 *sg. pret.* gebād WL 3, 3 *sg. pret.* R 9.

gebindan *sv.* 3 to bind ; 3 *sg. pret.* gebond R 19.

gebond *see* gebindan.

gebrǣcon *see* gebrecan.
gebrǣgd *see* gebregdan.
gebrecan *sv.* 5 to shatter ; 3 *pl.*
    pret. gebrǣcon R 1, *pp.* gebrocen
    R 32.
gebregdan *sv.* 3 to stimulate ; 3 *sg.*
    pret. gebrǣgd R 18.
gebrocen *see* gebrecan.
gecringan *sv.* 3 to fall down ; 3 *sg.*
    pret. gecrong R 31.
gecrong *see* gecringan.
gedǣlan *wv.* 1 to part ; 3 *sg. pret.*
    subj. gedǣlde WL 22.
gedreag *n.* multitude ; *acc. sg.* WL
    45.
gedrēas *see* gedrēosan.
gedrēosan *sv.* 2 to collapse ; 3 *sg.*
    pret. gedrēas R 11, *pp. nom. pl. f.*
    gedrorene R 5.
gedrorene *see* gedrēosan.
gefrǣtwan *wv.* 1 to adorn ; *pp.*
    gefrǣtwed R 33.
gegrunden *see* grindan.
gehātan *sv.* 7 to promise HM 11.
gehēawan *sv.* 7 to gash ; *pp.*
    gehēawen R 12.
gehrorene *see* hrēosan.
gehȳran *wv.* 1 to hear ; 1 *sg. pres.*
    gehȳre HM 50, 2 *sg. pret. subj.*
    gehȳrde HM 22.
gelāc *n.* rolling ; *acc. sg.* WL 7.
gelǣg *m.* expanse ; *acc. pl.* gelagu
    HM 42.
geleoran *sv.* 4 to pass away ; *pp.*
    nom. pl. m. geleorene R 7.
gelettan *wv.* 1 to hinder HM 25.
gelimpan *sv.* 3 to happen *HM* 30.
gelong *adj.* dependent ; *nom. sg. f.*
    WL 45.
gemǣc *adj.* suitable ; *acc. sg. m.*
    gemǣcne WL 18.
gemon *v.* I remember ; 3 *sg. pres.*
    WL 51, 2 *sg. pret. subj.* gemunde
    HM 14.
gemunde *see* gemon.
gemynd *n.* mind ; *dat. pl.* gemyn-
    dum HM 31.
genōh *adj.* enough ; *acc. sg. n.* HM 35.
geōmor *adj.* sad ; *nom. sg. m.* WL
    17, *acc. sg. m.* geōmorne HM 23,
    dat. sg. f. geōmorre WL 1.

geōmormōd *adj.* sober-minded ;
    nom. sg. m. WL 42.
geond *prep. w. acc.* throughout
    WL 36, *HM* 37.
geong *adj.* young ; *nom. sg. m.* WL
    42.
georn *adj.* eager ; *nom. sg. m.* HM
    43.
gēotan *sv.* 2 to pour R 42.
gerestan *wv.* 1 to rest WL 40.
gesēcan *wv.* 1 to seek out ; 1 *sg.*
    pret. gesōhte HM 6.
gesīþ *m.* companion ; *dat. pl.*
    gesīþum HM 34.
gesōhte *see* gesēcan.
gesprǣcon *see* gesprecan. ˙
gesprecan *sv.* 5 to agree upon ; 2
    pl. pret. gesprǣcon HM 16,
    gesprǣconn HM 54.
getwǣfan *wv.* 1 to divert HM 24.
geþōht *m.* thought ; *nom. sg.* WL
    43, *acc. sg.* WL 12.
geunne *see* geann.
gewāt *see* gewītan.
geweorc *n.* handiwork ; *nom. sg.* R 2.
gewidost *adv. superl.* as far apart
    as possible WL 13.
gewītan *sv.* 1 to depart ; 1 *sg. pret.*
    gewāt WL 9, 3 *sg. pret.* WL 6 ;
    3 *pl. pret.* gewitan R 9.
gewitloca *m.* mind ; *dat. sg.*
    gewitlocan HM 15.
giedd *n.* tale ; *acc. sg.* WL 1.
gīet *adv.* still R 12.
gif *conj.* if HM 48.
git *pron.* you two ; 2 *dual nom.*
    HM 16, 17, 33, 54, *gen.* incer HM
    49, *dat.* inc HM 32.
glǣdmōd *adj.* joyous ; *nom. sg. m.*
    R 33.
gleomu *f.* splendour ; *dat. sg.*
    gleoma R 33.
God *m.* God ; *nom. sg.* HM 32.
gold *n.* gold ; *gen. sg.* goldes *HM*
    36.
goldbeorht *adj.* bright with gold ;
    nom. sg. m. R. 33.
gongan *sv.* 7 to walk ; 1 *sg. pres.*
    gonge WL 35.
grimme *adv.* fiercely R 14.

grindan *sv.* 3 to sharpen ; *pp.* gegrunden R 14.

gripe *m.* grasp ; *nom. sg.* R 8.

habban *wv.* 3 to have WL 43, 3 *sg. pres.* hafað HM 35, 44, R 6, 1 *sg. pret.* hæfde WL 7.

hæf *n.* sea ; *acc. pl.* hafu *HM 8.*

hæfde *see* habban.

hæleþ *m.* man ; *gen. pl.* hæleþa HM 39.

hafað *see* habban.

hafu *see* hæf.

hār *adj.* grey ; *acc. sg. m.* hārne R 43.

hāt *adj.* hot ; *nom. pl. m.* hāte R 43, 45 *nom. pl. n.* hāt R 41.

hāt *n.* heat ; *dat. sg.* hāte R 38.

hātan *sv.* 7 to command ; 3 *sg. pret.* hēt WL 15, HM 13, heht WL 27, HM 20.

hē *pron. m.* he ; *nom sg.* WL 51, HM 31, 35, 48, 52, *acc. sg.* hine HM 19, *gen. sg.* his WL 46, *dat. sg.* him WL 45, HM 30, 45, 53 *nom. pl.* hȳ WL 12, *gen. pl.* hyra R 27.

hēah *adj.* high ; *nom. sg. n.* R 22, *acc. pl. n.* HM 8.

healdan *sv.* 7 to hold ; 3 *sg. pres. subj.* healde HM 37.

heard *adj.* steadfast, fierce ; *nom. sg. m.* WL 43, R 8.

heardsǣlig *adj.* ill-starred ; *acc. sg. m.* heardsǣligne WL 19.

heht *see* hātan.

heonan *adv.* from here WL 6, HM 27.

heorte *f.* heart ; *gen. sg.* heortan WL 43.

hēr *adv.* here WL 15, 32, HM 39, hither HM 8.

here *m.* army ; *nom. pl.* hergas R 29.

heeswēg *m.* martial noise ; *nom. sg.* R 22.

hēt *see* hātan.

hine, his, him *see* hē.

hit *pron. n.* it ; *nom. sg.* WL 24.

hlāford *m.* lord ; *nom. sg.* WL 6, 15.

hliþ *n.* hillside ; *gen. sg.* hliþes HM 22.

hof *n.* building ; *nom. pl.* hofu R 29.

hold *adj.* devoted ; *gen. pl. m.* holdra WL 17, *HM 39.*

horngestrēon *n.* abundance of gables ; *nom. sg.* R 22.

hrēorig *adj.* ruinous ; *nom. pl. m.* hrēorge R 3.

hrēosan *sv.* 2 to fall ; *pp. nom. pl. m.* gehrorene R 3.

hreþer *n.* heart ; *dat. sg.* hreþre R 41.

hrīm *m.* frost ; *nom. sg.* R 4.

hring *m.* circle ; *acc. pl.* hringas R 19.

hringmere *m.* circular pool ; *acc. sg.* R 45.

hrōf *m.* roof ; *nom. sg. R 31,* *nom. pl.* hrōfas R 3.

hrōstbēag *m.* circle formed by inner roofwork ; *gen. sg.* hrōstbēages R 31.

hrungeat *n.* barred gate ; *nom. sg.* R 4.

hrūse *f.* earth ; *acc. sg.* hrūsan R 29, *gen. sg.* R 8.

hryre *m.* ruin ; *nom. sg.* R 31.

hū *conj.* how HM 10, R 49.

hund *n.* hundred ; *nom. sg.* R 8.

hwǣr *conj.* where WL 8.

hwæt *pron.* which ; *acc. sg. n.* WL 3.

hwæt *interjection* lo ! HM 13.

hwætrēd *adj.* ingenious ; *nom. sg. m.* R 19.

hȳ *see* hē.

hycgan *wv.* 3 to think WL 11, 2 *sg. pres. subj.* hycge HM 11 ; intending *pres. p. acc. sg. m.* hycgendne *WL 20.*

hycgendne *see* hycgan.

hyge *m.* mind ; *nom. sg.* WL 17 ; *dat. sg.* HM 11.

hygegeōmor *adj.* sad at heart ; *acc. sg. m.* hygegeōmorne WL 19.

hygerōf *adj.* resolute ; *nom. sg. m.* R 19.

hyra *see* hē.

hȳþelic *adj.* convenient ; *nom. sg. n.* R 41.

ic *pron.* I ; *nom. sg. m.* HM 1, 2, 6, 11, 50, *nom. sg. f.* WL 1, 2, 3 (2X), 5, 7, 9, 16, 18, 25, 29, 35, 37, 38, 39 ; *acc. sg. m.* **mec** HM 3, 7, *acc. sg. f.* WL 14, 15, 27, 32, 41 ; *dat. sg. f.* **mē** WL 1, 9, 18, *dat. sg. m.* **mē** HM 31.

in *prep. w. acc.* into ; HM 3, R 19 ; *w. dat.* in WL 13, 28.

inc, incer *see* **git.**

is *see* **wesan.**

iū *adv.* formerly R 32.

lād *f.* course ; *acc. sg.* **lāde** HM 25.

lǣran *wv.* 1 to persuade *HM 21.*

lǣstan *wv.* 1 to carry out HM 53.

lǣtan *sv.* 7 to allow ; *imper. sg.* **lǣt** HM 24, 3 *pl. pret.* **lēton** R 42.

lagu *m.* sea ; *acc. sg.* HM 21.

lāmrind *f.* crust of mud ; *dat. pl.* **lāmrindum** R 17.

langoþ *m.* longing ; *gen. sg.* **longaþes** WL 41, *dat. sg.* **langoþe** WL 53.

lāðlicost *adv. superl.* in most wretched fashion WL 14.

lēas *adj.* devoid of ; *nom. sg. n.* WL 32.

leger *n.* bed ; *acc. pl.* WL 34.

lēode *m. pl.* people ; *dat.* **lēodum** WL 6.

lēodfruma *m.* lord ; *nom. sg.* WL 8.

lēof *adj.* loved (one) ; *gen. sg. m.* **lēofes** WL 53, *nom. pl. m.* **lēofe** WL 34, *gen. pl. m.* **lēofra** WL 16.

lēton *see* **lǣtan.**

līf *n.* life ; *dat. sg.* **līfe** WL 41.

lifdon, lifgende *see* **lifian.**

lifian *wv.* 3 to live ; 1 *pl. pret.* **lifdon** WL 14, *pres. p. acc. sg. m.* **lifgendne** HM 25, *dat. sg. m.* **lifgendum** HM 53, *nom. pl. m.* **lifgende** WL 34.

līm *m.* cement ; *dat. sg.* **līme** R 4.

lond *n.* land ; *acc. sg.* HM 18, *gen. sg.* **londes** WL 8, HM 4.

londstede *m.* country ; *dat. sg.* WL 16.

longaþes *see* **langoþ.**

longian *wv.* 2 *impers. w. acc. of person* to long ; 3 *sg. pret.* **longade** WL 14.

lustum *adv.* joyfully HM 21.

lȳt *adj. indecl. w. gen. pl.* few WL 16.

mā *adv.* to a greater degree WL 4.

mæg *v.* I can ; 1 *sg. pres.* WL 2, 38, 39, 3 *sg. pres.* HM 30.

mǣg *m.* kinsman ; *nom. pl.* **māgas** WL 11.

mǣw *m.* seagull ; *gen. sg.* **mǣwes** HM 26.

māgas *see* **mǣg.**

māra *see* **micel.**

māðum *m.* treasure ; *gen. pl.* **māðma** HM 46.

mē, mec *see* **ic.**

mearh *m.* horse ; *gen. pl.* **mēara** HM 46.

mengan *wv.* 1 to stir up, HM 44.

meododrēam *m.* festive joy ; *gen. pl.* **meododrēama** HM 46.

meodoheall *f.* mead-hall ; *nom. sg.* R 23.

meoduburg *f.* mead city ; *dat. pl.* **meoduburgum** HM 17.

mere *m.* sea ; *acc. sg.* HM 26.

merelād *f.* ocean track ; *acc. sg.* **merelāde** HM 28.

merestrēam *m.* ocean current ; *acc. pl.* **merestrēamas** HM 44.

micel *adj.* great ; *nom. sg. m.* R 22, *acc. sg. f.* **micle** WL 51, *comp. nom. sg. m.* **māra** HM 31.

mīn *adj.* my ; *nom. sg. m.* WL 6, 8, 15, 17, 47, 50, HM 7, 39, *gen. sg. m.* **mīnes** WL 26, HM 10, *gen. sg. f.* **mīnre** WL 2, 40, *dat. sg. f.* WL 10, *acc. pl. m.* **mīne** WL 38, *gen. pl. m.* **mīnra** WL 5.

mīþan *wv.* 1 to conceal ; *pres. p. acc. sg. m.* **mīþendne** WL 20.

mōd *n.* mind ; *nom. sg.* R 18, *acc. sg.* WL 20.

mōdcearu *f.* grief of heart ; *acc. sg.* **mōdceare** WL 51, *gen. sg.* WL 40.

mōdlufe *f.* heart's love ; *acc. sg.* **mōdlufan** *HM 10.*

mon *see* monn.

mondrēam *m.* revelry of men ; *gen. pl.* mondrēama R 23.

mondryhten *m.* liege lord ; *nom. sg.* HM 7.

monian *wv.* 2 to instigate ; 3 *sg. pret* monade *R 18.*

monig *adj.* many ; *nom. sg. m.* R 32, *nom. sg. f.* R 23, *nom. pl. m.* monige R 21.

monn *m.* man, one ; *nom. sg.* mon WL 27, 42, HM 44, *acc. sg.* monn HM 25, *gen. sg.* monnes WL 11.

monna *m.* man ; *acc. sg.* monnan WL 18, HM 28.

morþor *n.* crime, murder ; *acc. sg.* WL 20.

mōston *see* mōt.

mōt *v.* I may ; 1 *sg. pres.* WL 37, 3 *pl. pres.* mōtan HM 33, 2 *pl. pret.* mōston HM 17.

myne *m.* purpose ; *acc. sg.* R 18.

naca *m.* ship ; *acc. sg.* nacan HM 41.

næglian *wv.* 2 to stud ; *pp. acc. pl. m.* næglede HM 35.

ne *adv.* not WL 22, 39, 41, HM 24, 30, 46 (3X).

nēah *adv.* near WL 25.

nemne *conj.* except WL 22.

niman *sv.* 4 to take up WL 15.

nis *see* wesan.

nīwes *adv.* recently WL 4.

nō *adv.* not at all WL 4, 24.

nū *adv.* now WL 4, 24, HM 1, 8, 9, 20, 44.

nȳd *f.* necessity ; *dat. sg.* nȳde HM 41.

of *prep. w. dat.* from, out of WL 6, 53, HM 20.

ofer *prep. w. acc.* across, over, WL 7, HM 8, R 43, concerning HM 49 ; *w. dat.* beyond HM 28, on HM 47.

oferwinnan *sv.* 3 to overcome ; *pp.* oferwunnen HM 45.

oferwunnen *see* oferwinnan.

oflongian *wv.* 2 to seize with longing ; *pp.* oflongad WL 29.

ofstondan *sv.* 6 to remain standing ; *pp.* ofstonden R 11.

oft *adv.* often WL 21, 32, 51, HM 6, 16, 54, R 9.

on *prep. w. acc.* on to HM 42, 43, upon R 35(3X), 36(3X), 37 ; *w. dat.* in WL 16, 27, 35, 41, 50, HM 6, 9, 11, 15, 16, 17, 23, 29, 30, 31, 54, R 41, on WL 33, HM 22, R 4.

ond *conj.* and WL 14, HM 9, 34, 42, 51, 52, R 10, 30, 33, 34.

onginnan *sv.* 3 to begin ; 2 *sg. imper.* ongin HM 26, 3 *pl. pret.* ongunnon WL 11.

onhwēorfan *sv.* 2 to change ; *pp.* onhworfen WL 23.

onhworfen *see* onhwēorfan.

onsittan *sv.* 5 to board ; 2 *sg. imper.* onsite HM 27.

onsundran *adv.* apart HM 1.

onwendan *wv.* 1 to change ; 3 *sg. pret.* onwende R 24.

ōra *m.* edge ; *dat. sg.* ōran HM 22.

orþonc *m.* monument of skill ; *nom. sg.* R 16.

oþ *conj.* until R 8 ; *prep. w. acc.* up to R 45.

ōþer *adj.* another ; *dat. sg. n.* ōþrum R 10.

oþþæt *conj.* until R 24.

oþþe *conj.* or WL 4.

ōwiht *pron.* anything ; *nom. sg. n.* WL 23.

ræghār *adj.* grey with lichen ; *nom. sg. m.* R 10.

rēadfāh *adj.* stained with red ; *nom. sg. m.* R 10.

rīce *n.* kingdom ; *acc. sg.* R 10, *gen. sg.* rīces R 37.

sægde *see* secgan.

sǣnaca *m.* ship ; *acc. sg.* sǣnacan HM 27.

scān *see* scīnan.

sceādan *sv.* 7 to part ; 3 *sg. pres.* sceādeð R 30.

sceal *v.* I must ; 1 *sg. pres. WL* 25, 3 *sg. pres.* WL 43, 52, HM 3, 2 *sg. pres.* scealt HM 9, 3 *sg. pres. subj.* scyle WL 42, 3 *sg. pret.* sceolde HM 42.

sceard *adj.* gaping ; *nom. pl. f.* scearde R 5.

sceolde *see* sceal.

scieran *sv.* 4 to rend ; *pp. nom. pl. f.* scorene R 5.

scīnan *sv.* 1 to shine ; 3 *sg. pret.* scān R 15, 34.

scorene *see* scieran.

scūrbeorg *f.* protection from storms *nom. pl.* scūrbeorge R 5.

scyle *see* sceal.

sē *pron.* that ; *dat. sg. m.* þām WL 52, *nom. sg. n.* þæt WL 23, R 41, 48, *acc. sg. n.* WL 2, 11, R 24 ; *rel. nom. sg. m.* sē HM 13 ; *adj. nom. sg. m.* sē WL 50, HM 29, 44, R 49, *gen. sg. m.* þæs WL 11, 41, *nom. sg. f.* sēo R 12, 24, *acc. sg. f.* þā HM 52(2X) *gen. sg. f.* þēere WL 40, *acc. sg. n.* þæt R 45, *dat. sg. n.* þām WL 28, *nom. pl. n.* þā R 40, 46.

seah *see* sēon.

sealt *adj.* salt ; *acc. pl. m.* sealte HM 5.

searogim *m.* precious stone ; *acc. pl.* searogimmas R 35.

sēcan *wv.* 1 to seek WL 9, HM 26.

secg *m.* man ; *dat. pl.* secgum HM 34.

secgan *wv.* 3 to tell WL 2, HM 1 ; 3 *sg. pret.* sægde HM 31.

secgrōf *adj.* valiant ; *gen. pl. m.* secgrōfra R 26.

sēo *see* sē.

sēon *sv.* 5 to look ; 3 *sg. pret.* seah R 35.

settan *wv.* 1 to set HM 4.

sigeþēod *f.* powerful nation ; *dat. sg.* sigeþēode HM 20.

sinc *n.* treasure ; *acc. sg.* HM 34, R 35.

sinchroden *adj.* richly-adorned ; *nom. sg. f.* HM 14.

sind, sindon *see* wesan.

sinsorg *f.* constant sorrow ; *gen. pl.* sinsorgna WL 45.

sittan *sv.* 5 to sit *WL* 37 ; 3 *sg. pres.* siteð WL 47.

sīð *m.* lot, journey ; *acc. sg.* WL 2, *gen. sg.* sīþes HM 24.

sippan *adv.* afterwards HM 24, 33 ; *conj.* since WL 3, HM 22.

stān *m.* stone ; *acc. sg.* R 43.

stānhlip *n.* cliff ; *dat. sg.* stānhlipe WL 48.

stānhof *n.* stone building ; *nom. pl.* stānhofu R 38.

stēap *adj.* high ; *nom. sg. m.* R. 11.

stōdan *see* stondan.

stondan *sv.* 6 to stand ; 3 *pl. pret.* stōdan R 38.

storm *m.* storm ; *dat. sg.* storme WL 48, *dat. pl.* stormum R 11.

strēam *m.* stream ; *nom. sg.* R 38, *acc. sg. pl.* strēamas HM 5, R 43.

sumorlang *adj.* long as in summer ; *acc. sg. m.* sumorlangne WL 37.

sūð *adv.* southwards HM 27.

swā *conj.* as if WL 24.

swift *adj.* swift ; *acc. sg. m.* swiftne R 18.

swīpe *adj.* mighty ; *nom. sg. f.* R 24.

swylce *adv.* likewise WL 43.

swylt *m.* death ; *nom. sg.* R 26.

sȳ *see* wesan.

sylf *pron.* self ; 2 *nom. sg. f.* HM 14, *wk.* 3 *nom. sg. m.* sylfa HM 20, 1 *gen. sg. f.* sylfre WL 2, 3 *dat. sg. m.* sylfum WL 45.

sylfor *n.* silver ; *acc. sg.* R 53.

tēaforgēap *adj.* red curved ; *wk. nom. sg. m.* tēaforgēapa R 30.

tigel *f.* tile ; *dat. pl.* tigelum R 30.

tīrfæst *adj.* glorious ; *acc. sg.* tīrfæste HM 12.

tō *adv.* too WL 51 ; *prep. w. acc.* to R 29, *w. dat.* R 32.

tōdǣlan *wv.* 1 to part ; 3 *pl. pret. subj.* tōdǣlden WL 12.

tōgædre *adv.* together R 20.

torr *m.* tower ; *nom. pl.* torras R 3.

trēocyn n. species of tree ; *acc. sg.* HM 2.

trēow f. fidelity ; *acc. sg.* trēowe HM 12.

tūdor n. offspring ; *dat. sg.* tūdre HM 2.

twēgen *adj.* two ; *gen. pl. m.* twēga HM 49.

ðā *conj.* when WL 9 ; *adv.* then WL 18.

þā *see* sē.

þǣr *adv.* there HM 12, R 40 ; *conj.* where WL 37, 38, HM 7, 29, R 32, 46.

þēēre *see* sē.

þæs *see* sē *and* þes.

þæsþe *conj.* as HM 31.

þæt *conj.* that WL 12, 13, 22, 47, HM 12, 14, 21, 27, 33, 52.

þæt *pron. see* sē.

þām *see* sē.

þās *see* þes.

þē *see* þū.

þe *pron. indecl.* who, which WL 41, 52, HM 16, 54.

þēahþe *conj.* although HM 39.

þec *see* þū.

þenden *conj.* while HM 17.

þēoden m. prince ; *nom. sg.* HM 29, *gen. sg.* þēodnes HM 48.

þes *adj.* this ; *nom. sg. m.* WL 29, R 1, þæs R 9, 30, *acc. sg. m.* þisne HM 13, *dat. sg. m.* þissum WL 16, *acc. sg. f.* þās R 37, *acc. sg. n.* þis WL 1, *dat. sg. n.* þissum WL 41, *nom. pl. n.* þās R 29, *acc. pl. n.* WL 36.

þis, þisne, þissum *see* þes.

þīn *see* þū.

þing n. thing ; *nom. sg.* R 48.

þon *see* ēac.

þonne *adv.* then HM 13, R 42, 47 ; *conj.* than WL 4, HM 32 ; when WL 35.

þū *pron.* you ; *2 sg. nom. f.* HM 10, 12, 14, 21, 22, 24, 27 ; *acc.* þec HM 13, 24 ; *gen.* þīn HM 29, 48, *dat.* þē HM 1, 20.

þurh *prep. w. acc.* through WL 12.

ūhte f. period before dawn ; *dat. sg.* ūhtan WL 35.

ūhtcearu f. grief before dawn ; *acc. sg.* ūhtceare WL 7.

unc, uncer *see* wit.

under *prep. w. dat.* beneath WL 28, 36, 48, R 11.

underetan *sv.* 5 to undermine ; *pp. nom. pl. f.* undereotone R 6.

ūp *adv.* up WL 3.

ūphēah *adj.* lofty ; *nom. pl. f.* ūphēa WL 30.

ūt *adv.* outwards HM 41.

wā *interjection* woe! WL 52.

wæl n. slaughtered man ; *nom. pl.* walo R 25.

wēr f. pledge *acc. sg.* wǣre HM 52.

wǣre, wǣron, wǣs *see* wesan.

wæter n. water ; *dat. sg.* wætre WL 49.

wāg m. wall of a building ; *nom. sg.* R 9.

waldendwyrhta m. master builder ; *acc. pl.* waldendwyrhtan R 7.

walo *see* wæl.

wēa m. woe ; *acc. pl.* wēan HM 45.

weal m. wall ; *nom. sg.* R 39.

weallwala m. foundation ; *acc. pl.* weallwalan R 20.

wealstān m. masonry ; *nom. sg.* R 1.

weardigan *wv.* 2 to occupy HM 18 ; *3 pl. pres.* weardiað WL 34.

wearp *see* weorpan.

wēaþearf f. grievous need ; *dat. sg.* wēaþearfe WL 10.

wēn f. expectation ; *dat. pl.* wēnum HM 29.

weorpan *sv.* 3 to gush ; *3 sg. pret.* wearp R 38.

weorþan *sv.* 3 to become ; *3 pl. pret.* wurdon R 27.

wēpan *sv.* 7 to weep WL 38.

wer m. man ; *gen. pl.* wera R 26.

wērigmōd *adj.* disconsolate ; *nom. sg. m.* WL 49.

werþēod f. people ; *gen. pl.* werþēoda R 9.

wesan v. to be WL 42 ; 1 *sg. pres.*
eom WL 29, HM 8, 3 *sg. pres.*
bið WL 52, **is** WL 17, 23, 24, 29,
HM 29, R 1, 47, 48, **nis** HM 45,
3 *pl. pres.* **sind** WL 33, R 3,
sindon WL 30 ; 3 *sg. pres. subj.*
sȳ WL 45, 46 ; 3 *sg. pret.* **wæs**
R 41, 3 *pl. pret.* **wǣron** R 21,
40, 46 ; 3 *sg. pret. subj.* **wǣre**
WL 8, 24.

wēstenstaþol m. deserted place ;
acc. pl. **wēstenstaþolas** R 27.

wīc n. abode ; *nom. sg.* WL 32,
acc. pl. WL 52.

wid *adj.* broad ; *wk. dat. sg. m.*
widan R 39.

wide *adv.* far and wide WL 46, R
25.

wīghyrst f. war trappings ; *dat. pl.*
wīghyrstum R 34.

wīgsteal n. bastion ; *nom. pl.* R 27.

willa m. desire ; *nom. sg.* HM 30,
gen. pl. **wilna** HM 45.

willan v. to wish ; 1 *sg. pres.*
wille HM 1, 3 *sg. pret.* **wolde** HM
53.

wine m. friend, lover ; *nom. sg.*
WL 49, 50, HM 39.

winelēas *adj.* friendless ; *nom. sg.*
m. WL 10.

winetrēow f. pledge of fidelity ;
acc. sg. **winetrēowe** HM 52.

wīngāl *adj.* flushed with wine ;
nom. sg. m. R 34.

winnan *sv.* 3 to suffer ; 1 *sg. pret.*
wonn WL 5.

wīr m. metal rod ; *dat. pl.* **wīrum**
R 20.

wit *pron.* we two ; 1 *dual nom.*
WL 13, 21, *acc.* **unc** WL 12, 22,
gen. **uncer** WL 25.

wīte n. torment ; *acc. sg.* WL 5.

wlonc *adj.* proud ; *nom. sg. m.* R
34.

wōldæg m. day of pestilence ; *nom.
pl.* **wōldagas** R 25.

wolde *see* **willan.**

wong m. ground ; *acc. sg.* R 31.

wonn *see* **winnan.**

wordbēotung f. promise ; *gen. pl.*
wordbēotunga HM 15.

wōrian *wv.* 2 to moulder ; 3 *sg.
pres.* **wōrað** R 12.

woruld f. world ; *gen. sg.* **worulde**
WL 46, *dat. sg.* HM 30.

woruldrīce n. whole world ; *dat.
sg.* WL 13.

wræcca m. wanderer ; *nom. sg.*
WL 10.

wræcsīð m. misery ; *acc. pl.*
wræcsīðas WL 38, *gen. pl.*
wræcsīða WL 5.

wrǣtlic *adj.* wondrous ; *nom. sg.
m.* R 1.

wrāþe *adv.* fiercely WL 32.

wrecan *sv.* 5 to utter ; 1 *sg. pres.*
wrece WL 1.

wudu m. wood ; *gen. pl.* **wuda** WL
27.

wundrum *adv.* wonderfully R 20.

wunian *wv.* 2 to dwell WL 27.

wurdon *see* **weorþan.**

wylm m. surge ; *dat. sg.* **wylme** R
39.

wyn f. joy ; *nom. sg.* WL 46, *gen. pl*
wynna WL 32.

wynlic *adj* delightful ; *comp. wk.
acc. pl. n.* **wynlicran** WL 52.

wyrd f. fate, event ; *nom. sg.* R 24,
nom. pl. **wyrde** R 1.

ymb *prep. w. acc.* concerning HM
10.

yrmþu f. hardship ; *gen. pl.*
yrmþa WL 3.

ȳþ f. wave ; *gen. pl.* **ȳþa** WL 7,
HM 42.

Printed and bound by CPI Group (UK) Ltd, Croydon, CR0 4YY

14/04/2025

14656917-0001